Collins

OCR GCSE 9-1

Computer Science

Revision Guide

Paul Clowrey

How to use this Revision & Practice book

Revise

These pages provide a recap of everything you need to know for each topic.

You should read through all the information before taking the Quick Test at the end. This will test whether you can recall the key facts.

Practise

These topic-based questions appear shortly after the revision pages for each topic and will test whether you have understood the topic. If you get any of the questions wrong, make sure you read the correct answer carefully.

Review

These topic-based questions appear later in the book, allowing you to revisit the topic and test how well you have remembered the information. If you get any of the questions wrong, make sure you read the correct answer carefully.

Mix it Up

These pages feature a mix of questions for the different topics. They will make sure you can recall the relevant information to answer a question without being told which topic it relates to.

Test Yourself on the Go

Visit our website at **collins.co.uk/collinsGCSErevision** and print off a set of flashcards. These pocket-sized cards feature questions and answers so that you can test yourself on all the key facts anytime and anywhere. You will also find lots more information about the advantages of spaced practice and how to plan for it.

Workbook

This section features even more topic-based questions as well as practice exam papers, providing two further practice opportunities for each topic to guarantee the best results.

ebook

To access the ebook, visit **collins.co.uk/ebooks** and follow the step-by-step instructions.

QR Codes

Found throughout the book, the QR codes can be scanned on your smartphone for extra practice and explanations.

A QR code in the Revise section links to a Quick Recall Quiz on that topic. A QR code in the Workbook section links to a video working through the solution to one of the questions on that topic.

Contents

Computer Systems

Contents

The Purpose and Function of the Central Processing Unit

You must be able to:

- Describe the purpose of the Central Processing Unit (CPU)
- Describe common CPU components and their function
- Describe the main concepts of von Neumann architecture.

What is the Central Processing Unit For?

- The **central processing unit (CPU)**, also known as a microprocessor, is the 'brain' at the core of any computer system.
- All computer systems have the following three basic elements:
    1. **Input** – data feeds into the system from **input devices** such as a keyboard or mouse, webcam or sensor.
    2. **Process** – the data collected needs to be processed and actions need to be carried out. This may mean carrying out calculations, sending instructions to other devices or transferring data from different areas of memory.
    3. **Output** – once processed or acted on, the result is presented via **output devices** such as a display, speaker, printer or automated manufacturing equipment.
- The CPU is where this processing takes place, and modern processors are based on **von Neumann architecture** or structure.

Common Central Processing Unit Components

- Modern CPUs contain the following key elements:
    - The **arithmetic logic unit (ALU)** is where calculations are carried out. These include mathematical tasks, logic tests and data comparisons.
    - The **control unit** controls the flow of data around the system, both inside the CPU and between input and output devices. Control signals are sent to the ALU, cache and memory registers.
    - **Cache** is a small area of very fast memory within the CPU used to store frequently and recently used data and instructions. A CPU **register** is a quickly accessible memory location within the processor. Registers either store memory locations or the actual data to be processed.

Key Point

A smart touchscreen tablet is an example of both an input (finger-touch control) and output device (LED screen).

Key Point

The CPU processes data and instructions, and coordinates the flow of data around a system.

von Neumann Architecture

- The original design on which most modern computers are based was created by mathematician **John von Neumann** in 1945.
- The diagram shown below is based on his design for a 'stored program' computer system. This means that both the computer program and the data it processes are stored in memory.

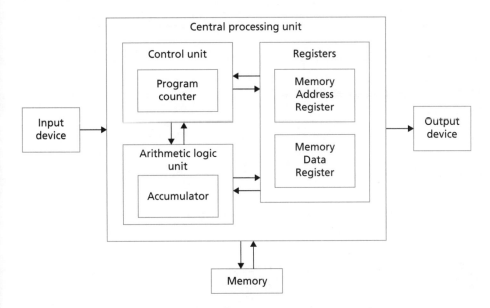

- Key aspects of von Neumann architecture include:

  - **Memory Address Register** (MAR): this is the location address in memory of the next piece of data or instruction that the CPU needs to be fetched or stored.
  - **Memory Data Register** (MDR): an instruction or piece of data fetched from memory is stored here temporarily until it is used.
  - **Program counter**: this continuously provides the CPU with the memory address of the next instruction in the cycle to be fetched.
  - **Accumulator**: this is where the results of calculations carried out by the ALU are temporarily stored until they are needed.
  - **Bus**: a physical pathway shared by signals to and from components of a computer system such as input and output devices; the arrows in the diagram represent wires and circuit boards.

Key Words

central processing unit
input devices
output devices
von Neumann architecture
arithmetic logic unit
control unit
cache
register
Memory Address Register
Memory Data Register
program counter
accumulator
bus

Quick Test

1. Which key element of the CPU carries out logic tests?
2. State one purpose of a 'register'.
3. Name four input devices.

Systems Architecture

Quick Recall Quiz

You must be able to:

- Explain the process of fetching and executing instructions
- Explain how the characteristics of a CPU affect its performance
- Describe the purpose and give examples of embedded systems.

The Fetch–Decode–Execute Cycle

- The fetch–decode–execute cycle, often referred to as just the fetch–execute cycle, describes how the CPU:
  1. fetches instructions
  2. decodes them
  3. carries out (or executes) the instructions.

Fetch: The processor fetches the instruction from memory and uses the program counter to keep track of where it is.

Execute: The instruction is then carried out; this could be a calculation or the transfer of data.

Decode: Once the instruction is loaded, the CPU needs to know what it means, so the instruction must be decoded.

Common Central Processing Unit Characteristics

- The performance of a CPU can be affected by several elements:
  - clock speed
  - cache size
  - number of **cores**.
- **Clock speed** refers to the rate at which instructions are processed by the CPU.
  - A 3-GHz (gigahertz) CPU can perform three billion cycles per second.

> **Key Point**
>
> An older CPU was primarily defined by its clock speed. In a modern CPU, the cache size and number of cores is just as important.

- **Cache size** – cache memory stores frequently and recently used data and instructions. The CPU processes instructions faster than they could be fetched from RAM so having them in cache memory means that the CPU is not sitting idle. This allows temporarily stored data to be accessed very quickly:
  - Modern CPUs may have two or more levels of cache, and once these have been used the CPU will then use the computer's main memory, which is much slower.
  - The L1 cache is used to store very frequently accessed data – it is quite small but very fast.
  - The L2 cache is slower and further away but is still more efficient than the main memory.
- **Number of cores** – rather than continuously increase the speed of a single processor, modern CPUs now contain multiple processors on the same chip. This is referred to as a multicore processor, and each core can carry out separate tasks simultaneously.

Number of cores	Name
2 cores	Dual core
4 cores	Quadcore
6 cores	Hexacore
8 cores	Octacore

What are Embedded Systems?

- A dedicated computer system, or multiple systems, programmed with a specific task within a larger device is an **embedded system**. Examples include:
  - a smartphone/smartwatch
  - the program control of a dishwasher or microwave
  - the installable apps and Internet functionality included in light emitting diode (LED) smart televisions
  - navigation, entertainment or engine management systems within a car.
- Designed to carry out a task over and over, embedded systems often have low power requirements and low maintenance.
- Although designed to last, embedded systems are often installed deep within the larger system and if they do fail can be difficult to replace or repair.

> **Quick Test**
>
> 1. What is the speed of a CPU measured in?
> 2. How does a multicore CPU help a computer to run faster?
> 3. For each of the following, name a device and a potential embedded system:
>   a) Kitchen appliance
>   b) Entertainment device

Key Point

Multicore processors have more than one processor on the same CPU.

Key Point

Embedded systems can be found within electronic devices that have multiple functions.

Key Words

clock speed
cores
embedded system

Memory

Quick Recall Quiz

You must be able to:

- Explain the need for primary storage
- Understand the difference between RAM and ROM
- Describe the purpose of RAM and ROM in a computer system
- Explain the need for virtual memory.

What is Primary Storage and Why Do We Need It?

- **Primary storage** describes the main memory components of a computer system.
- Also referred to as main memory, it is essential for storing data and processes being carried out by the CPU.
- Primary storage is normally located on the motherboard and normally includes RAM, ROM and CPU cache.

What are Random Access Memory and Read-Only Memory?

- **RAM** (random access memory) is a temporary area that a computer uses to store data in current use:
  - It is much quicker to access than the computer's hard drive.
  - It acts like our short-term memory, quickly recalling important information.
  - The two types of RAM are DRAM (dynamic RAM) and SRAM (static RAM).
- **ROM** (read-only memory) provides a computer system with important instructions that do not change. The instructions are permanently programmed into a chip and will have specific functions.

What is the difference between Random Access Memory and Read-Only Memory?

- Both RAM and ROM are stored on chips within the computer system, but there are key differences between them:
  - RAM is **volatile**, meaning that once power is switched off all data stored on it is lost.
  - ROM **permanently** stores the instructions written at manufacture.
  - RAM is read/write; ROM is read only.
  - Access to ROM is much slower than access to RAM.
  - RAM storage capacity is usually in the order of gigabytes.
  - ROM storage capacity is much smaller.

> **Key Point**
>
> Primary storage describes the main memory components of a computer system.

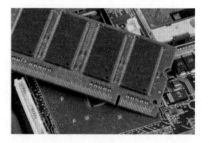

> **Key Point**
>
> SRAM is faster than DRAM but more expensive.

> **Key Point**
>
> RAM is volatile; ROM is permanent (or non-volatile).

Why Does a Computer System Need Random Access Memory and Read-Only Memory?

- When browsing the Internet, playing games or performing calculations, instructions and stored data need to be accessed quickly and RAM is much quicker to access than the hard drive.
- Data and instructions that are currently in use are stored in RAM. Placed in known storage locations by the CPU, they can be accessed in any order (hence 'Random Access Memory'), speeding up the system.
- When a computer starts, or boots, the first set of instructions accessed is the **BIOS** (basic input/output system) and this is stored within ROM. The BIOS ensures that all essential hardware can communicate effectively and launch the operating system.
- Because ROM is **non-volatile**, manufacturers place important instructions on it to ensure that these cannot be edited when the BIOS is used.

What is Virtual Memory?

- Running multiple applications on a modern computer system (e.g. office-based tasks, browsing and playing music) will quickly fill the RAM.
- If the RAM becomes full, the system will slow, so **virtual memory** is created using spare memory on the hard drive.
- Part of the hard drive memory is designated as temporary RAM, or virtual memory, and non-essential data stored in RAM is transferred to the hard drive.
- As access to the hard drive memory is slower than access to RAM, the system will slow if it is relied on too heavily.

> **Quick Test**
>
> 1. Does a computer system use RAM or ROM for the temporary storage of data?
> 2. Why will a system create virtual memory?
> 3. Essential system start-up instructions are normally stored in which area of primary storage?

> **Key Words**
>
> **primary storage**
> **RAM**
> **ROM**
> **volatile**
> **BIOS**
> **non-volatile**
> **virtual memory**

Storage Types, Devices and Characteristics

You must be able to:

- Describe the need for secondary storage
- Explain the term 'data capacity'
- Describe common types of storage media and devices and their characteristics
- Explain the most suitable choice of storage device for a given application.

What is Secondary Storage and Why Do We Need It?

- Away from the CPU and motherboard, secondary storage refers to the devices used to store programs, documents and files.
- These devices need to be non-volatile, otherwise we would need to install programs every time we wanted to use them.
- Data is stored magnetically, optically or electronically using a solid state drive (SSD).

> **Key Point**
>
> Non-volatile secondary storage means that data is still intact when the power source is removed.

Data Capacity and File Size

- The choice of secondary storage depends on the capacity of the device compared with the file size of the data to be stored.
- Common storage capacities are given in the tables on the next page and are based on the following units of measurement:

– 1 binary digit	=	1 bit
– 4 bits	=	1 nibble
– 8 bits	=	1 byte
– 1000 bytes	=	1 kilobyte (KB)
– 1000 kilobytes	=	1 megabyte (MB)
– 1000 megabytes	=	1 gigabyte (GB)
– 1000 gigabytes	=	1 terabyte (TB)
– 1000 terabytes	=	1 petabyte (PB)

- Please note that you may also see sizes referred to as 1024 rather than 1000. This is because 1024 is a power of 2 in relation to binary calculations.

> **Key Point**
>
> Although visually very similar, optical discs come in many different formats.

Secondary Storage Media Characteristics

- When comparing secondary storage, the following characteristics should be considered:
  - **Capacity** – How much data can be stored on each particular device?
  - **Speed** – How quickly can data be accessed? (read/write)
  - **Portability** – How easily can the device be moved from one location to another?
  - **Durability** – Can the drive be easily damaged in use?
  - **Reliability** – How long will the drive last? Do errors often occur?
  - **Cost** – How does the price per gigabyte compare to other devices?

Magnetic storage	Common applications	Advantages
	• Ideal for fixed location desktop PCs • Used as larger network storage and backup systems • Ideal for larger document files • Typical capacity: 1–5 TB	• High capacity at a low cost • Fast data access **Disadvantages** • The disk will eventually fail • Easily damaged, resulting in corruption of data • Large physical size • Complex moving parts increases power requirements

Optical storage	Common applications	Advantages

	• Ideal for portable systems
	• Often used for storing commercial and personal music, video and games
	• Wide range of capacities:
	  – CD (compact disc) 700 MB
	  – DVD (digital versatile disc) 4.7–9.4 GB
	  – Blu-ray 25–128 GB
		• Cheap to manufacture
		• Very portable
		• Widely available
		
		Disadvantages
		• Discs can be damaged easily and degrade over time
		• Limited capacity
		• Compatibility issues between players

SSD (solid state drive) storage	Common applications	Advantages

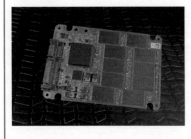	• Becoming the first choice of technology manufacturers, SSD storage is ideal for portable devices including:
	  – USB portable drives
	  – smartphone and tablet memory
	  – digital camera and video camera memory
	  – laptop and notepad computer memory
	  – games console memory expansion
	  – high-end desktop computers
		• Use significantly less power than magnetic hard drives
		• Faster read/write access than magnetic storage
		• Small size
		• No moving parts
		• Ideal for USB (Universal Serial Bus) and other portable devices
		
		Disadvantages
		• More expensive per GB than magnetic or optical storage
		• Can wear out over time
		• Capacity typically less than 2 TB

Quick Test

1. Give three reasons why games consoles use optical discs to store games.
2. Why is a magnetic hard drive not very durable?
3. Name five portable uses of SSDs.

Key Words

secondary storage
storage capacity
network storage

Units and Formats of Data

You must be able to:

- Explain why a computer can process data only in a binary format
- Describe common units of data
- Describe how binary codes are used to represent characters
- Explain the term 'character set'
- Describe the relationship between character bits and sets.

Binary and Units of Data

- Computers communicate and process instructions using binary. Each single character or set of instructions must be converted into a series of 0s and 1s that represent electrical flow (0 = off, 1 = on).
- As we do not speak binary and computers cannot be programmed without it, all instructions must be translated.
- Common units of data are shown in the table below:

> **Key Point**
>
> One numerical character = 1 byte (8 bits).

Name	Size	Typical examples
Bit (b)	1 binary digit	0 or 1
Nibble	4 bits	Half an 8-bit sequence, used in hexadecimal
Byte (B)	8 bits	Large enough to store one character (F, for example)
Kilobyte (KB)	1000 bytes	Small documents and text files
Megabyte (MB)	1000 kilobytes	Computer documents, music files and images
Gigabyte (GB)	1000 megabytes	High-resolution videos and games
Terabyte (TB)	1000 gigabytes	Capacity of large backup storage drives
Petabyte (PB)	1000 terabytes	International cloud storage systems

MEMORY UNITS

byte (B)			
KB kilobyte	**MB** megabyte	**GB** gigabyte	**TB** terabyte
PB petabyte	**EB** hexabyte	**ZB** zettabyte	**YB** yottabyte

> **Key Point**
>
> Consider a page of A4 text containing 3000 characters. Using standard 8-bit characters, this could create a 3000-byte file (or 3 kilobytes, KB).

Character Sets

- Communicating and programming in binary is extremely difficult and time-consuming.
- **Character sets** were created to bridge the gap, allowing alphanumeric characters that we recognise to be typed into a computer and converted into a usable binary equivalent.
- Each character set has been designed to follow a logical sequence. For example, 'D' in a character set is one higher than 'C'.
- Common character sets include:
  - **ASCII** (American Standard Code for Information Interchange), which was created to allow computer manufacturers in the English-speaking world to share a common coding standard. Originally a 7-bit code with 128 possible characters, an extra zero (bit) was added to the start of every binary sequence to create an 8-bit (1-byte) character set.

Key Point

Take a look at the full ASCII table online. You will not be expected to memorise these tables for the exam.

Key Point

Unicode also includes emojis!

Sample from ASCII table

ASCII Number	8-Bit Binary	Character
120	01111000	x
121	01111001	y
122	01111010	z
123	01111011	{
124	01111100		
125	01111101	}
126	01111110	~

ASCII character groups

ASCII Range	Value or Function
0–32	Unprintable control codes
33–47	Symbols and punctuation
48–57	Digital 0–9
58–64	More symbols
65–90	Upper-case letters A–Z
91–96	More symbols
97–122	Lower-case letters a–z
123–127	More symbols

- **Unicode**, an international encoding standard, was developed when it became clear that many more than 128 characters would be required for languages around the world. It is now a world industry standard. Unlike ASCII, Unicode has 8-bit, 16-bit and 32-bit variants.
- Unicode-32 can encode over 4 billion characters, allowing for every current and future language.

Key Point

Unicode was developed to set worldwide common coding standards.

Quick Test

1. How many bits are there in a nibble?
2. Why was an extra zero added to the original ASCII code?
3. How many characters can 8-bit ASCII represent?

Key Words

character sets
ASCII
Unicode

Converting Data 1

You must be able to:

- Convert denary numbers into binary numbers
- Perform simple binary calculations
- Explain the terms 'binary overflow' and 'binary shift'.

Quick Recall Quiz

Converting Denary into Binary

- **Denary**, or decimal, is our standard number system. It is a **base 10** system with 10 digits (0, 1, 2, 3, 4, 5, 6, 7, 8, 9).
- **Binary** is a **base 2** number system and is the language of computers. Each number in the table below represents one binary bit, so this is referred to as an **8-bit** structure:

128	64	32	16	8	4	2	1

- An 8-bit structure replaces each number with a binary switch (1 or 0, on or off).
- The sequence 00000001 would generate a total of 1.
- The sequence 11111111 would generate a total of 255.
- Using each binary switch, we can represent the denary numbers 0–255 (256 characters) as binary numbers and vice versa:
  - Converting denary into binary:
    198 = 11000110 (128 + 64 + 0 + 0 + 0 + 4 + 2 + 0)
  - Converting binary into denary:
    01010001 = 81 (0 + 64 + 0 + 16 + 0 + 0 + 0 + 1)

> **Key Point**
>
> Denary is another word for decimal.

Binary Calculations

- Binary numbers can be added together. For example, to work out the following:
  - 01010011 + 01110110
  - Work from the right and use these four rules, carrying under to the left as required:

Rule One:	0 + 0 = 0
Rule Two:	1 + 0 = 1
Rule Three:	1 + 1 = 10 (binary for 2)
Rule Four:	1 + 1 + 1 = 11 (binary for 3)

```
  0 1 0 1 0 0 1 1          83
+ 0 1 1 1 0 1 1 0        +118
  ─────────────          ────
  1 1 0 0 1 0 0 1         201
    1 1 1   1 1
```

Binary Overflow

- 8-bit binary has a maximum value of 11111111 (255).
- Anything over this value, for example 278, will produce an **overflow error**.
- This is because all 8 bits have been used and there is nowhere for the additional digit to be stored or handled.

Binary Shift

- When working directly with binary numbers, a **binary shift** to the left and right can be used for multiplication and division, respectively.
  - A **left shift** will multiply a binary number by 2^N (where N is the number of shifts to the left).

  For example, a left shift of 1 (binary number $\times 2^1$):

  0 0 1 0 1 1 0 0 (44)
  0 1 0 1 1 0 0 0 (88)

  - A **right shift** will divide a binary number by 2^N (where N is the number of shifts to the right).

  For example, a right shift of 1 (binary number $\div 2^1$):

  0 0 1 0 0 1 1 0 (38)
  0 0 0 1 0 0 1 1 (19)

Significant Bits

- The **most significant bit** (MSB) has the largest value and is the first number on the left. For example:
  - The MSB of the binary number 10000000 is 1 with a value of 128.
- The **least significant bit** (LSB) has the lowest value and is the first number on the right. For example:
  - The LSB of the binary number 00000001 is 1 with a value of 1.

Revise

Key Point

With a maximum denary value of 255, 8-bits can represent 256 characters.

Key Point

Modern computers are normally based around 32-bit or 64-bit systems. You are only expected to calculate values in 8-bit as part of your GCSE.

Key Point

Binary numbers with 1 to 7 bits work in exactly the same way. For example, 10110 (5-bit) is the same as 00010110 (8-bit).

Key Words

denary
base 10
binary
base 2
8-bit
overflow error
binary shift
most significant bit
least significant bit

Quick Test

1. Convert 196 into binary.
2. What is an overflow error?
3. Multiplying a binary number by four will require a left shift of . . .?

Converting Data 2

You must be able to:

- Convert binary numbers into hexadecimal numbers
- Convert hexadecimal numbers into denary numbers.

Hexadecimal

- **Hexadecimal** is a convenient way for programmers to express large binary numbers.
- Computers do not understand hexadecimal; it is simply a shortcut reference for programmers.
- It is a **base 16** number system and uses digits and letters.
  - Remember, binary is base 2 (two digits: 0, 1).
  - Denary is base 10 (10 digits: 0, 1, 2, 3, 4, 5, 6, 7, 8, 9).
  - Hexadecimal is base 16 (16 digits and letters: 0, 1, 2, 3, 4, 5, 6, 7, 8, 9, A, B, C, D, E, F).
  - The use of letters prevents the duplication of numbers.

> **Key Point**
>
> Photo-editing software will normally allow colours to be referenced in hexadecimal.

Converting Binary into Hexadecimal

- One hexadecimal digit can be used to represent a **nibble** (4 bits), meaning that two digits can represent one byte (8 bits).
- For example:

| 0 | 1 | 1 | 0 | 1 | 0 | 1 | 1 |

The 8-bit sequence is divided into two 4-bit nibbles:

| 0 | 1 | 1 | 0 | | 1 | 0 | 1 | 1 |

Converted into separate denary numbers:

6   **11**

Represented in hexadecimal using the table shown:

6B

- Confusion can occur when the hexadecimal number contains two numbers and no letters. For example, the binary number 00110110 becomes 36 in hexadecimal. This is stated as 'three-six' in hexadecimal, not 'thirty-six'.

Base 2 binary	Base 10 denary	Base 16 hexadecimal
0000	0	0
0001	1	1
0010	2	2
0011	3	3
0100	4	4
0101	5	5
0110	6	6
0111	7	7
1000	8	8
1001	9	9
1010	10	A
1011	11	B
1100	12	C
1101	13	D
1110	14	E
1111	15	F

Converting Hexadecimal into Denary

- Converting hexadecimal into denary involves converting each digit into its denary equivalent, multiplying by its base 16 position using the table below and adding the values together.

16^1	16^0
16	1

- Using the example of 6F:
  - Convert each digit into its denary equivalent (6 is represented by 6) and (F is represented by 15):
  - $6F = (6 \times 16^1) + (15 \times 16^0)$
  - $6F = (96) + (15)$
  - $6F = 111$

Uses of Hexadecimal

- As a shortcut reference for programmers, hexadecimal is used in a number of ways including:
  - Colour codes for over 16 million colours are referenced using hexadecimal.
  - A hexadecimal code is used to represent the MAC address, or physical address, of a computer component.
  - Error messages are presented in a hexadecimal code that refers to the memory location of the operating system error.

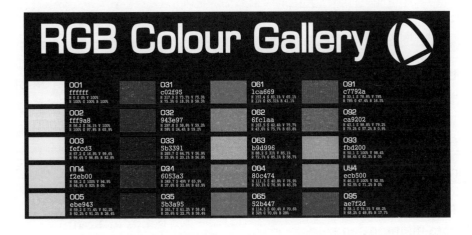

RGB Colour Gallery

Quick Test

1. Convert 00110101 into hexadecimal.
2. Convert 13A into denary.
3. How many nibbles make up an 8-bit binary sequence?

Key Words

hexadecimal
base 16
nibble

Audio/Visual Formats and Compression

You must be able to:

- Describe how images can be represented in binary
- Explain the terms 'metadata', 'colour depth' and 'resolution'
- Describe how sound can be stored digitally
- Explain the terms 'sampling', 'bit depth' and 'sample rate'
- Describe audio/visual compression techniques.

Images and Binary

- Images saved electronically are made up of a series of pixels – tiny squares in neat lines. Changing the colour or brightness of each pixel is what generates detail.
- All computer data is binary, and an image can be converted into binary by using a binary code to represent each pixel.

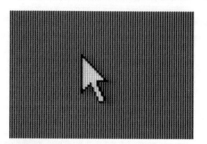

> The example below uses only two colours, each represented using 0 or 1.
> - 1-bit image: two colours (1^2), 0 or 1
> - 2-bit image: four colours (2^2), 00, 01, 10 and 11
> - More colours can be added using longer binary codes.

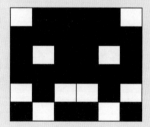

0	1	1	1	1	0
1	1	1	1	1	1
1	0	1	1	0	1
1	1	1	1	1	1
0	1	0	0	1	0
1	0	1	1	0	1

Key Point

Increasing the colour depth or resolution will improve the visual quality, but also the file size, of an image.

- **Colour depth** is the number of bits per pixel. A 4-bit image has 16 colours (2^4). Most modern devices use a 24-bit colour depth (2^{24}), with 16,777,216 colours.
- The more pixels used to create an image, the more detail displayed and the higher the **resolution**.
- An image file size is determined by its size in pixels and by the colour depth.
- In addition to the image itself, information can be stored within the same file. This **metadata** might include:
  - Technical data generated by the camera – image properties, aperture and shutter speed, resolution, **GPS location**, date and time.
  - Data added manually by the user – place names or captions, comments or people's names, the name of the photographer's business or copyright information.

For example, consider a 24-bit image of 800 × 600 pixels:
- 800 × 600 = 480,000 pixels
- 480,000 × 24 bits = 11,520,000 bits
- 11,520,000 ÷ 8 (8 bits in 1 byte) = 1,440,000 bytes or 1.44 megabytes.

Key Point

Modern cameras and smartphones add GPS location data as metadata.

Sound

- Live sound, recorded by a microphone, is called **analogue** sound.
- It is continuously changing and has many complex variables.

- To store sound on a computer, it must be converted into a digital file and stored as binary. This is called **sampling**.
- Sampling records and measures the sound at regular time intervals throughout the duration of the audio clip. The number of samples taken each second is the **sample rate**.
- As the sample rate increases, so does the quality of the sound file.
- The **bit depth** is the number of bits used to encode the sample.
- Recording duration is normally measured in seconds.
- For example, consider a 4-minute (240 seconds) stereo music track with a standard sample rate:
  - 240 × 44,100 × 16 = 169,344,000 bits
  - 169,344,000 × 2 (stereo tracks) = 338,688,000 bits
  - 338,688,000 bits ÷ 8 (8 bits in 1 byte) = 42,336,000 bytes or 42,336 MB.

Key Point

Increasing the sample rate or bit depth of a recording increases the playback quality but also the file size. Increasing the duration also increases the file size.

Compression

- High definition video, graphical and audio files have large file sizes. As we store more and more data, **data compression** can be used to reduce large file sizes. There are several benefits of data compression:
  - Storage space required on mobile devices and home computers can be reduced.
  - Smaller files can be uploaded and downloaded more quickly.
  - Limits placed on file sizes by streaming and email services can be avoided.
- The balance between quality and file size, especially with audio and visual data, has led to the creation of different compression methods:
  - **Lossy compression** removes data, for example duplicated elements, to create a smaller file size. Any data removed during the compression is removed permanently.
    - Popular lossy file types include JPEG, MP3, GIF and MP4.
  - **Lossless compression** uses software algorithms to compress data but then reconstructs it into its original form, preserving the original file.
    - Popular lossless file types include RAW, WAV, TIFF and BMP.

Key Point

Compact discs have a sample rate of 44,100 or 44.1 kHz (kilohertz) and a bit depth of 16. Remember, audio file sizes should then be doubled if in stereo.

File Size Calculation Recap

- Resulting file sizes are in bytes.
  - text file = bits per character × number of characters
  - sound file = duration (s) × sample rate × bit depth
  - image file size = image height × width (pixels) × colour depth

Key Words

colour depth
resolution
metadata
GPS location
analogue
sampling
sample rate
bit depth
data compression
lossy compression
lossless compression

Quick Test

1. An image file is made up of 17,488,000 bits. How many megabytes is this?
2. Name a music file format that uses a high level of compression.
3. A music producer is creating master copies of a new track. Which compression method should they use and why?

The Purpose and Function of the Central Processing Unit

1 Which part of the body is the CPU often compared to? _____ **[1]**

2 For each device, place a tick in **one** of the columns to indicate whether the device feeds into the CPU or receives instructions from it. **[6]**

Device	Input	Output
Keyboard		
Printer		
Monitor		
Webcam		
Sensor		
Speakers		

3 In which CPU component are calculations carried out? _____ **[1]**

4 What is the small area of very fast memory within the CPU known as? _____ **[1]**

5 Describe the control unit. **[1]**

_____

6 Define the term 'stored program'. **[2]**

_____

_____

7 Name the **two** registers within the von Neumann model. **[2]**

_____

8 Complete the following sentence:

The area within the ALU that stores the results of calculations until needed is called the

_____. **[1]**

9 Which aspect of von Neumann architecture continuously provides the CPU with the memory address of the next instruction? **[1]**

_____

10 In which decade was the von Neumann design created? _____ **[1]**

Systems Architecture

1 Match each term with its description. **[3]**

Fetch	The instruction is decoded to enable it to be understood
Decode	The instruction is carried out
Execute	The instruction is brought from memory

2 CPU clock speed is measured in _____. **[1]**

3 How many cores does a quadcore processor have? _____ **[1]**

4 Which is faster, the L1 cache or the L2 cache? _____ **[1]**

5 A 2-GHz CPU will carry out how many cycles per second when processing instructions? **[1]**

6 What is the main benefit of multicore processors? **[1]**

7 List **three** devices that may contain an embedded system. **[3]**

8 Describe a potential use for an embedded system in:

a) a smart TV **[1]**

b) a washing machine. **[1]**

Memory

1 What do the abbreviations RAM and ROM stand for? **[2]**

2 Which of RAM and ROM is a temporary storage area? **[1]**

3 Which of RAM and ROM permanently holds specific functions? **[1]**

4 Define the term 'volatile memory'. **[2]**

5 Which of RAM and ROM is volatile? **[1]**

6 *Access to ROM is slower than access to RAM.* True or false? **[1]**

7 What does the abbreviation BIOS stand for? **[1]**

8 When is the BIOS normally accessed? Tick **one** box.

   A When a new program is installed. ☐

   B When the computer boots up. ☐

   C As the computer shuts down. ☐ **[1]**

9 When is virtual memory needed? **[1]**

10 Why is virtual memory slower than standard RAM? **[1]**

11 *RAM, ROM and cache are considered primary storage.* True or false? **[1]**

Storage Types, Devices and Characteristics

1 Why does secondary storage need to be non-volatile? **[1]**

2 List **three** methods of storing data. **[3]**

3 1000 megabytes is called a .... **[1]**

4 *When using units of bytes it is commonly accepted that the '24' can be ignored and*

that data capacities are described to the nearest 1000. True or false? .... **[1]**

5 Put the following in order of size, from smallest to largest: **TB, KB, GB, MB** **[1]**

6 List **six** characteristics used to compare secondary storage devices. **[6]**

7 Which type of optical storage has a standard range of capacities of 4.7–9.4 GB? **[1]**

8 Which storage type is the most expensive per GB? .... **[1]**

9 State **two** reasons why SSDs are ideal for portable USB devices. **[2]**

10 Describe **two** considerations to be made when storing important files for long periods of time. **[2]**

11 Name the most common type of storage in desktop computers. _____ **[1]**

Units and Formats of Data

1 A modern office considering a backup system would most likely need it to have a capacity in the order of which size? Tick the correct answer.

  A Kilobytes ☐

  B Terabytes ☐

  C Nibbles ☐ **[1]**

2 How many bits would be required to save the word 'data' in 8-bit ASCII? _____ **[1]**

3 How many gigabytes is 6144 MB equal to? _____ **[1]**

4 Briefly describe the term 'character set'. **[2]**

_____

_____

5 What is the abbreviation ASCII short for? **[1]**

_____

6 How many characters did the original ASCII set represent? **[1]**

_____

7 Why was an extra bit added to the original ASCII binary equivalent? **[2]**

_____

_____

8 Name the worldwide character set designed to represent all known languages. **[1]**

_____

Converting Data 1

1 State the number base system of the following.

   a) Denary .... [1]

   b) Binary .... [1]

2 Convert the following binary numbers into denary.

   a) 00000001 .... [1]

   b) 11111111 .... [1]

   c) 10110101 .... [1]

   d) 00110011 .... [1]

   e) 01010101 .... [1]

   f) 11110000 .... [1]

3 Add the following binary numbers: 10110101 and 00110011 [1]

4 What is the highest possible 8-bit binary value and why? [2]

5 Briefly describe the term 'binary overflow'. [1]

6 What would be the effect on a binary number of:

   a) a left shift of 1? [1]

   b) a right shift of 1? [1]

Converting Data 2

1. List the 16 digits in the base 16 number system. [1]

2. Complete the sentence:

   The primary purpose of hexadecimal for programmers is [1]

3. Why are letters used in the hexadecimal system? [1]

4. Convert the following binary numbers into hexadecimal.

   a) 00110001 [1]

   b) 10101101 [1]

   c) 01111110 [1]

   d) 11100001 [1]

5. Convert the following hexadecimal numbers into denary.

   a) 6D [1]

   b) 3B [1]

   c) 75 [1]

6. How many bits does a nibble represent? [1]

Audio/Visual Formats and Compression

1 Match each term with its definition. **[3]**

Metadata	The number of bits per pixel.
Colour depth	The number of pixels per inch used to create an image.
Resolution	Additional information saved within the image file.

2 List in binary the **four** colours of a 2-bit image. **[4]**

3 How many pixels would form a mobile phone screen with a resolution of 1334 × 750? **[1]**

4 Calculate the file size of a mono audio track of 3 minutes with a standard sample rate of 44,100 and a bit depth of 16. **[1]**

5 Explain why recording at a higher sample rate will create a larger digital audio file. **[1]**

6 Describe a potential danger of using image compression. **[1]**

7 List **three** popular compressed file types used to store sound or images. **[3]**

8 *Lossy compression can never be returned to its original state once saved.* True or false? **[1]**

Wired and Wireless Networks 1

You must be able to:

- Explain the difference between wired and wireless networks
- Describe different types of network.

How are Networks Formed?

- Linking together computer devices so that they can communicate and exchange information is what forms a **network**.
- Desktops, laptops, tablets, printers, smart TVs and smartphones can all connect to a network, and the Internet is built on many networks connected using cables and wireless technology.

Local Area Network

- A local area network (LAN) consists of computers and peripheral devices connected in a small geographical area such as a school or an office building.
- Each computer or device can run independently but can exchange information through switches.

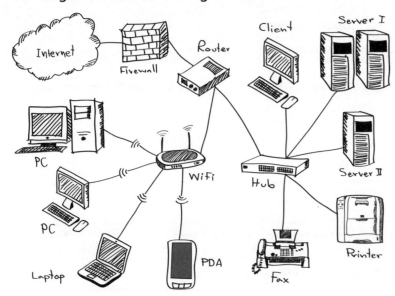

A LAN

Key Point

Connecting multiple LANs together using a router forms a WAN.

Wide Area Network

- Connecting one LAN to another, or multiple LANs over a large distance, forms a wide area network (WAN).
- A WAN may span across the globe using telephone lines, fibre-optic undersea cables and even satellites.
- The largest WAN today is the Internet.

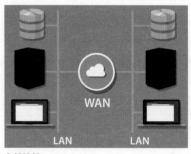

A WAN

What Affects the Performance of a Network?

- The number of devices on the same network will affect the performance as the bandwidth must be shared between all of the users of the same network, lowering everyone's connection speed.
- **Bandwidth**, measured in bits per second (bps), is the amount of data that can pass between two network devices per second.
- There are several other factors that can affect the performance, and potential bandwidth speed, of a network:
  - The quality of the transmission media, either wired or wireless.
  - There can be interference from external factors, such as distance, and other electronic devices, such as microwaves.

Bandwidth

What is a Client–Server Network?

- A **client–server** network is when a main computer **server** (that controls access to the files and data it stores) is accessed from multiple **client** computers.
- This allows security, user access and backups to be carried out by the central server.

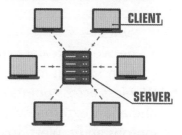

CLIENT-SERVER NETWORK

CLIENT

SERVER

What is a Peer-to-Peer Network?

- All computers within a **peer-to-peer** network (P2P) act as both client and server – they share files, programs and network access.
- Security **permissions** are shared across the network, and a user can access the contents of any other user's computer on the same network.
- Lack of any central control means data can be added or deleted by any user of the network.
- It is important that all peer-to-peer users check their individual network security settings.

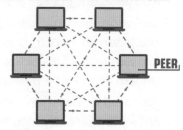

PEER-TO-PEER (P2P) NETWORK

 PEER

> **Key Point**
>
> Peer-to-peer networks are often associated with piracy and illegally sharing files as there is no central control.

> **Quick Test**
>
> 1. Why would an international bank use a WAN?
> 2. What security issues may arise from connecting to a peer-to-peer network?
> 3. Name three factors that can affect the performance of a network.

> **Key Words**
>
> LAN
> WAN
> bandwidth
> client–server
> server
> client
> peer-to-peer
> permissions

Quick Recall Quiz

Wired and Wireless Networks 2

You must be able to:

- Describe the devices used to connect computers to a network
- Explain how networks link across the world, forming the Internet.

Network Hardware

- In addition to a stand-alone computer, common network hardware includes:
  - wireless access points
  - routers
  - switches
  - network interface controllers/cards (NICs)
  - transmission media.
- **Wireless access points** are devices that connect to a network and allow external wireless devices, such as smartphones, laptops and tablets, to connect to that network.
- **Routers** connect networks together. This connection may be between multiple LANs to create a WAN or between a LAN and the Internet (which is a much larger network).
- **Network switches** act as a gateway between computers, allowing information to be passed between them and sent directly to a specified destination **media access control** (MAC) address.
- **NICs** plug directly into the motherboard of a desktop computer and allow the computer to communicate with a network using either an Ethernet cable or wireless technology.
  - Each NIC includes a MAC address that provides a unique identifier within a LAN.
  - In newer computers and laptops, NIC functionality is usually built into the motherboard rather than on a separate card.
- **Transmission media** is the term used to describe how network devices are connected to each other, using either cables or wireless communication.
  - Wired networks traditionally use copper wire Ethernet cables to transmit data between devices, up to a maximum of 100 metres.
  - Fibre-optic cables (which transmit data as flashes of light) have been used for larger networks requiring bigger bandwidths over longer distances.
  - Wireless technology (often referred to as Wi-Fi) uses radio waves to transmit data between compatible routers and computers.
  - Wireless networks also include 3G and 4G mobile phone networks and Bluetooth.

> **Key Point**
>
> Every network-compatible device has a permanent MAC address to identify it on a network.

> **Key Point**
>
> MAC addresses are stored as 12-digit hexadecimal numbers. For example, 00-5F-1B-68-E2:39

Global Networks and the Internet

- The Internet is a vast interconnected collection of all of the network technologies described in this chapter.
- The World Wide Web (WWW), proposed by Tim Berners-Lee in 1990, utilises this technology to publish pages written in HyperText Markup Language (HTML), which can be viewed using a web browser anywhere in the world.
- The Domain Name Service (DNS) is an Internet naming service that links the Internet Protocol (IP) address of a computer on a network to a text-based website address that is easier to remember (for example www.collins.co.uk). It is made up of multiple Domain Name Servers around the world.
- Hosting means allowing users to access a specific computer – the host – via a network connection.
  - The host may be an individual computer, local server or web server anywhere in the world; it must be constantly running and maintained so that users can always access it.
  - Web-hosting companies follow this process on a much larger scale, renting space on their network for individuals and organisations to host their own websites.
  - It is possible to run a hosting computer at home, but a high level of technical knowledge is required.
- Cloud computing allows Internet users not only to access remote files but also to run applications such as word processers, graphics software and even games directly from a remote server without the need to install them locally.

Key Point

In order to build Internet connections across the world, fibre optic cables have been laid on ocean floors.

Advantages of Cloud Computing	Disadvantages of Cloud Computing
• Software can be run within a browser, removing the need for remote updates. • Not location based, ideal for remote or home working. • Collaboration possible from multiple locations. • Remote back-ups can be regularly made. • Cloud services can be accessed via desktop and smart devices. • Previous versions of changed documents can usually be accessed if needed.	• Without Internet access, files or programs cannot be accessed. • Increased risk of security concerns, hacking, or questions of data ownership. • Storage capacity can be limited/expensive, depending on the provider. • Downtime – a cloud service may stop working, meaning work cannot be accessed. • Many professional cloud services are subscription-fee based.

- A web server stores and hosts websites, and controls client access to specific (usually HTML format) web pages stored upon it. This requested information is then rendered in the client web browser.
- A file server network provides shared access to files hosted on a specific network computer that all network users can access.

Key Words

routers
switches
media access control
Domain Name Service
Internet Protocol
Domain Name Server
hosting
cloud computing
web server
file server

Quick Test

1. What device is required to connect LANs together as a WAN?
2. What service links IP addresses and website names?
3. List five uses of cloud computing.

Network Topologies

You must be able to:

- Explain the term 'network topology'
- Describe star and mesh topologies.

What is a Network Topology?

- A **network** **topology** is the arrangement of computers and network devices in either a physical or a logical topographical structure.
- There are many configurations, each with associated advantages and disadvantages.
- Two common network topologies are named star and mesh.
- Network-compatible technology includes routers and switches, desktop computers, laptops, printers, smartphones, tablets and storage devices.
- Each device at an intersection/connection point is referred to as a node.

> **Key Point**
>
> A **node** is any device connected within a network.

Connecting Computers in a Star Topology

- At the centre of a **star network** is a server.
- Each compatible device has its own connection to the server.
- The server directs data transmissions between devices on the network.

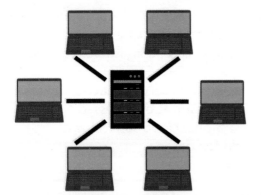

Advantages and Disadvantages of a Star Network

Advantages	Disadvantages
• The failure of one device, as long as it is not the server, will not affect the rest of the network. • The network can be expanded by adding devices until the server capacity is reached. • Localised problems can be identified quickly. • Data can be directed to a specific address via the central server – this reduces network traffic.	• If the server fails, then the whole network will collapse. • Extensive cabling and technical knowledge is needed to maintain the server.

Connecting Computers in a Mesh Topology

- In a **mesh network**, every device within the network is connected to every other device.
- Network traffic is shared between all devices.

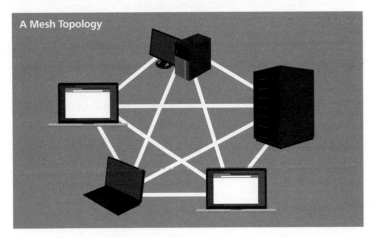

A Mesh Topology

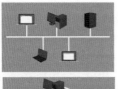
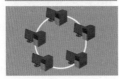
Advantages and Disadvantages of a Mesh Network

Advantages	Disadvantages
- All devices share the network load, helping the network to run smoothly. - If one device fails, the network will continue to run, as all of the devices are connected to all of the other devices. - Adding more devices will not affect the speed of the network.	- Managing the network requires a high level of network expertise. - The network can be expensive to set up because of the number of devices required.

Typical Network Layouts

This table shows some typical network scenarios.

Scenario	Topology	Reason for choice
A home network with multiple devices	Star network	The router can centrally link all wired and wireless devices and share access to the Internet.
The Internet	Mesh network	Any Internet-connected device around the world can contact another device via multiple smaller networks without a direct link.
Company with two offices in different cities	Each has a star network	The router in each star network provides access to the Internet and allows two networks to talk to each other.

Quick Test

1. How are devices connected in a mesh network?
2. What happens if the server fails in a star network?
3. Give four examples of a network node.

Protocols and Layers

Quick Recall Quiz

You must be able to:

- Describe wired and wireless modes of connection
- Explain the need for Wi-Fi encryption
- Describe why IP and MAC addresses are used
- Describe the need for hardware and software standards
- Describe network protocols and the concept of layers.

Modes of Connection

- A **wired** connection between devices describes a physical connection. The most common is an **Ethernet** cable, which is used to connect NICs, routers and switches and can handle data up to 100 gigabits per second (Gbps).
- A **wireless** connection describes the use of radio waves to transmit a signal or message between compatible devices.
    - Modern devices, containing **Wi-Fi-certified** chips, connect to a wireless local area network (WLAN) broadcast signal between 2.4 and 5GHz.
    - **Bluetooth** is a short-range, wireless, personal network technology standard (approx. 10 m). It is used primarily with wireless speakers, headphones, games controllers and other peripherals.

The Need for Encryption

- To prevent unauthorised external access, Wi-Fi networks use **encryption** and require a user to enter a password to connect.
- Current Wi-Fi encryption standards include:
    - **Wired Equivalent Privacy** (WEP) – the oldest and least secure standard. It can be easily hacked and is not recommended for modern devices.
    - **Wi-Fi-Protected Access** (WPA, WPA2 and WPA3) – combines encryption with a secure password to protect WLAN access. WPA3 is the most recent and most secure.

The Concept of Network Addresses

- IP addresses (for example 172.16.1.40):
    - are assigned to network devices to allow data transfer across the Internet using the Transmission Control Protocol (TCP)/IP
    - are described as **static** if permanently assigned to a key network device
    - are described as **dynamic** if assigned by the router within a network and can change each time the network is restarted
    - are normally stored as four denary numbers.

Key Point

WLAN is short for wireless local area network.

Key Point

Modern Ethernet variants include Cat 5 and Cat 6, using twisted pairs of wire.

Key Point

Wi-Fi-certified devices have been designed to work on common Wi-Fi networks anywhere in the world.

Key Point

From motherboards and smart speakers to device chargers, new devices must conform to hardware standards.

Hardware and Software Standards

- We can only use operating systems and applications across multiple devices because manufacturers and program developers conform to certain agreed **standards**.
  - **Hardware standards** include, but are not limited to, common interface or charging sockets, motherboard compatibility and communication connectivity.
  - **Software standards** include, but are not limited to, common file types, operating systems and web browsing formats.

Key Point

A new digital audio file, web page or smartphone game must be designed to meet software standards.

Network Protocols

- To allow network devices from worldwide manufacturers to communicate effectively, they must follow rules (**protocols**).

Key Point

Without HTTPS, online transactions would not be secure.

Protocol	Description
TCP/IP	A set of protocols that allow computers on multiple networks, including the Internet, to transmit and receive data packets.
HTTP (Hypertext Transfer Protocol)	Rules followed by web servers and web clients, or browsers, which host and present websites based on our requests.
HTTPS (HTTP Secure)	HTTP Secure encrypts communication between server and client. This makes secure online shopping and banking possible.
FTP (File Transfer Protocol)	Used to connect clients and servers across a network to exchange files. Traditionally used to upload files to a web server.
POP (Post Office Protocol)	Used to log in to and retrieve email messages from a mail server. When connected, all messages are downloaded to that device.
IMAP (Internet Message Action Protocol)	Allows access to an email server but, rather than downloading messages, they are simply read. This allows synchronised access from multiple devices, unlike POP.
SMTP (Simple Mail Transfer Protocol)	Used to send email messages to an email server rather than to receive messages.

The Concept of Layers

- The term 'layers' refers to a set of protocols with specific functions.
- Data can be transmitted between adjacent layers.

Layer Name	Description and Relevant Protocols
Application layer	Data relevant to web browsers and email clients – includes HTTP, FTP and SMTP.
Transport layer	Ensures that data is sent and received correctly between network hosts – includes TCP.
Internet (or network) layer	Communicates the IP addresses of all devices used in data traffic between network routers – includes IP.
Data link layer	Concerned with physical data transfer over cables – includes Ethernet.

Key Words

wired
Ethernet
wireless
Wi-Fi-certified
Bluetooth
encryption
Wired Equivalent Privacy
Wi-Fi-Protected Access
standards
hardware standards
software standards
protocols
layers

Quick Test

1. Why are hardware standards important?
2. Which email protocol would an online-based email service use?

The Purpose and Function of the Central Processing Unit

1 Name the **three** common elements of all computer systems. **[3]**

2 A robotic arm in a manufacturing plant would be an _____ device. **[1]**

3 Which component of the CPU stores recently and frequently used instructions? **[1]**

4 What does the abbreviation ALU stand for? **[1]**

5 What area of the CPU directs the flow of data around the system? **[1]**

6 What term is used to describe a physical pathway shared by signals to and from components of a computer system? **[1]**

7 Within von Neumann architecture, what is a key difference between the MDR and MAR functions? **[1]**

8 What is the purpose of the MDR? **[1]**

9 In which area of the von Neumann architecture is the accumulator found? **[1]**

10 Which area of the von Neumann architecture holds the memory location address of the next piece of data required? **[1]**

Systems Architecture

1 In the fetch–decode–execute cycle, in which area is an instruction carried out? **[1]**

2 *The CPU has its own memory storage*. True or false? _____ **[1]**

3 Complete the sentence:

For the CPU to understand the instructions fetched from memory, they must be

_____. **[1]**

4 Complete the paragraph below using the words from the box. **[4]**

| slower | very fast | more efficient | L1 cache |

_____ is used to store very frequently accessed data. It is quite small but

_____. The L2 cache is _____ and further away but still

_____ than the main memory.

5 *Modern CPUs can have more than two levels of cache*. True or false? _____ **[1]**

6 What **three** characteristics define the performance of a CPU? **[3]**

7 How many cores do the following processors have?

a) 2-GHz hexacore _____ **[1]**

b) 3-GHz quadcore _____ **[1]**

c) 2-GHz single core _____ **[1]**

d) 4-GHz dualcore _____ **[1]**

e) 2-GHz octacore _____ **[1]**

8 Define the term 'embedded system'. **[2]**

Memory

1 RAM is sometimes referred to as being like which of the following? Tick **one** box. **[1]**

A Our long-term memory ☐   **B** Our short-term memory ☐   **C** Our permanent memory ☐

2 Which of RAM and ROM has the smaller storage capacity? .... **[1]**

3 What feature of ROM allows instructions to be written to it when it is manufactured? **[1]**

4 Give **two** reasons why a CPU uses RAM rather than the computer hard drive for short-term calculations. **[2]**

5 Where is BIOS data stored? **[1]**

6 Is virtual memory created to support RAM or ROM? .... **[1]**

7 Where is virtual memory created? **[1]**

8 List **three** areas of primary storage. **[3]**

9 Why do some smartphones allow SD cards to be used to expand on-board memory? **[2]**

Storage Types, Devices and Characteristics

1 Secondary storage refers to storage not contained within which **two** computer components? **[2]**

_____

2 What does the abbreviation SSD stand for? _____ **[1]**

3 How many bits make up 1 byte? _____ **[1]**

4 A terabyte is how many megabytes? _____ **[1]**

5 Match each prefix with its definition. **[4]**

kilo		million

mega		trillion

giga		thousand

tera		billion

6 What is the most common storage media for physically purchasing console games? **[1]**

_____

7 Which type of storage has many complex moving parts? **[1]**

_____

8 List **two** advantages and **two** disadvantages of optical storage. **[4]**

_____

_____

_____

_____

9 Name **three** types of optical disc. **[3]**

_____

10 Why might replacing a magnetic hard drive in a laptop with an SSD make it run faster? **[1]**

11 Early portable MP3 players had small magnetic hard drives. What was a common problem with them? **[1]**

Units and Formats of Data

1 Suggest a suitable size for a memory card holding 300 MP3 files (around 3 MB each). **[1]**

2 Half an 8-bit sequence is called what? Tick the correct answer.

A Byte ☐   **B** Binary digit ☐   **C** Nibble ☐   **[1]**

3 *The ASCII character set was originally based on the English language alphabet*. True or false? **[1]**

4 Complete the ASCII table below. **[3]**

ASCII	8-Bit Binary	Character
120		x
121	01111001	
	01111010	z

5 Briefly describe the purpose of Unicode. **[2]**

6 Complete the following sentence:

Unprintable control codes and upper-case letters A–Z are examples of .... **[1]**

Converting Data 1

1 Denary and _____ are interchangeable terms. **[1]**

2 List the first eight place values in base 2. **[1]**

3 Convert the following denary numbers into binary using 8-bit only.

a) 60 _____ **[1]**

b) 189 _____ **[1]**

c) 40 _____ **[1]**

d) 11 _____ **[1]**

e) 257 _____ **[1]**

f) 99 _____ **[1]**

4 How many shifts to the left would be required to multiply a binary number by 4? **[1]**

5 Carry out a left shift of 3 on the binary number 00011010. Show the new binary number and the denary equivilent before and after the shift. **[3]**

6 Why is the highest value in 8-bit binary 255 and not 256? **[1]**

Converting Data 2

1 Hexadecimal is a base _____ number system. [1]

2 How many hexadecimal digits are used to represent 1 byte? [1]

3 Convert the following hexadecimal numbers into binary.

a) 8B _____ [1]

b) 11 _____ [1]

c) 3F _____ [1]

d) F2 _____ [1]

4 Two hexadecimal digits can be used to represent how many nibbles? _____ [1]

5 *A computer can read hexadecimal without translation.* True or false? [1]

6 Convert the following denary numbers into hexadecimal.

a) 199 [1]

b) 50 [1]

c) 242 [1]

Audio/Visual Formats and Compression

1 Images are made up of tiny squares known as _____. [1]

2 Using two-colour binary (0 = white, 1 = black), create a binary sequence to represent the image shown. [2]

3 List **three** pieces of information that can be found in image metadata. [3]

4 How many colours does an 8-bit image contain? [1]

5 Calculate the file size of an 8-bit image with a resolution of 800 × 600 pixels. [3]

6 Name the process of converting analogue sound into a digital format. [1]

7 Briefly describe the term 'audio sample rate'. [1]

8 Describe **three** benefits of audio/visual data compression. [3]

9 Why might lossless compression be popular with film editors? [2]

Computer Networking

Practice Questions

Wired and Wireless Networks 1

1 List **five** network-compatible devices. [5]

2 What do the abbreviations LAN and WAN stand for? [2]

3 What is often referred to as the largest WAN today? [1]

4 The performance of a network can be affected by several elements. Name **three** of these elements. [3]

5 Describe a client–server network. [3]

6 A popular network for sharing media across the Internet is called a [1]

7 Bandwidth is measured in .... [1]

8 Describe a common security concern of using peer-to-peer networks. [1]

9 Undersea network cables usually use which type of technology? [1]

Wired and Wireless Networks 2

1. The abbreviation NIC stands for .... [1]

2. List **three** types of wireless connectivity. [3]

   ....

   ....

   ....

3. What device is normally used to connect LANs together? [1]

   ....

4. What does the abbreviation MAC stand for? [1]

   ....

5. Name the service linking an IP address and a website address. [1]

   ....

6. The abbreviation IP stands for .... [1]

7. Complete the following paragraph using the words in the box. [4]

Internet	applications	cloud computing	remote

   .... allows .... users not only to access

   .... files but also to run .... such as word processors,

   graphics software and even games.

8. Which programming language is commonly used to create web pages? [1]

   ....

9. Briefly describe the process of commercial web hosting. [3]

   ....

   ....

   ....

Network Topologies

1 List **two** network topologies. **[2]**

2 What device would normally be at the centre of a star network? **[1]**

3 Describe **two** advantages and **two** disadvantages of a star network. **[4]**

4 *If a device fails in a mesh network, the network will fail*. True or false? **[1]**

5 The Internet is structured around which topology? **[1]**

6 Why would a mesh network require more cabling than a star network? **[1]**

7 Describe the term 'node'. **[1]**

Protocols and Layers

1 Why is encryption important when using Wi-Fi? **[2]**

2 Why is WEP not currently recommended for use? **[2]**

_____

_____

3 List **three** network protocols. **[3]**

_____

4 Name the term used to describe a set of protocols with specific functions. **[1]**

_____

5 Which protocol allows secure online shopping to take place? **[1]**

_____

6 Uploading files to a web server would use which protocol? **[1]**

_____

7 Match each term with its description. **[4]**

Application layer	Concerned with physical data transfer over cables
Transport layer	Communicates the IP addresses of devices between routers
Internet (or network) layer	Data relevant to web browsers and email clients
Data link layer	Ensures that data is correctly sent and received between network hosts

8 Cat 5 and Cat 6 are common types of _____. **[1]**

9 What do the abbreviations TCP/IP stand for? **[1]**

_____

Common System Threats

You must be able to:

- Describe a variety of common threats to computer networks
- Describe the potential dangers of each threat
- Explain how criminals exploit our trust to access information.

Why are Networks Attacked?

- Computer networks are part of our homes, schools, and places of work and leisure.
- Personal, business and financial information is extremely valuable and is traded between criminals around the world.
- Stolen usernames and passwords allow criminals to access bank accounts and private information, which means that they can potentially commit crimes against us without our knowledge.

> **Key Point**
>
> Personal information and passwords are traded across the world by criminals wanting to access our online accounts.

Malware

- **Malware** is short for 'malicious software', and describes a piece of software designed to breach security or damage a system.
- Types of malware include:

Virus	A program hidden within another program or file, designed to cause damage to file systems.
Worm	A malicious program that acts independently and can replicate itself to spread between multiple connected systems.
Trojan	Installed by a user thinking it is a legitimate piece of software when, in fact, it will cause damage or provide access for criminals.
Spyware	Secretly passes information on to a criminal without the user's knowledge. It is often packaged with free software.
Adware	Displays targeted advertising and redirects search requests without permission.
Ransomware	Limits or denies a user access to their system until a ransom is paid to unlock it.
Pharming	The redirecting of a user's website – by modifying their Domain Name Server (DNS) entries – to a fraudulent site without their permission.

> **Key Point**
>
> Recent victims of large-scale ransomware attacks include the National Health Service (NHS), UK universities and international school website providers. In each case, payment was demanded to restore access to data locked by the cyber-criminals.

Social Engineering

- Throughout history, con artists have tried to trick people into giving up personal information or valuables.
- We, as computer users, are seen by attackers as the 'weak point' of any system.

- These **social engineering** methods have developed into computer-based scams that prey on the good nature of users and pretend to be from a trusted organisation or contact.
    - **Phishing** uses email, text messages and phone calls to impersonate, for example, a financial organisation and ask users to confirm or divulge personal details. These details can be used to access and steal from online accounts. Most organisations have now agreed never to add click links within messages or contact users directly to confirm personal information.
    - **Shouldering** is the technique of watching a user at an ATM (automated teller machine) (cash machine) and recording their PIN (personal identification number) details.
    - **Blagging** is carried out face to face and uses believable scenarios to trick people into giving up personal information.

Threats Aimed Directly at Large Networks

- Large organisations and businesses are often the victims of attacks that try to access their computer systems to steal large quantities of data or inflict major damage.
    - A **brute force attack** repeatedly tries different usernames and passwords in an attempt to access a system.
    - A **denial of service (DoS) attack** tries to flood a website or network with data traffic to bring it to a halt. Such attacks are often used to demand a ransom or a change in policy.
    - **Data interception and theft** is the method of intercepting and decoding a message containing sensitive information before it reaches its destination.
    - **SQL injection** uses the same Structured Query Language used to manage large databases to attack them. Commands written in this language are used instead of usernames and passwords to access and steal private information.

 Quick Test

1. Name five types of malware.
2. What is shouldering?
3. What tips would you offer to someone using an ATM for the first time?
4. What does 'DoS attack' stand for?

Key Point

Scams are not just limited to traditional email, but can also be sent to our smartphones and tablets using voice calls, SMS and instant messages.

Key Words

malware
virus
worm
Trojan
spyware
adware
ransomware
pharming
social engineering
phishing
shouldering
blagging
brute force attack
denial of service (DoS) attack
data interception and theft
SQL injection

Threat Prevention

Quick Recall Quiz

You must be able to:

- Describe how users and organisations can prevent threats
- Explain how networks can be tested to identify potential threats
- Describe how to increase system security and the importance of strong passwords.

How Can We Protect Ourselves?

- The protection of our computer systems has to constantly evolve to meet the ever-increasing number of threats.
- The threats are from various sources, such as computer users with criminal intent and automated self-replicating virus programs.
- Threats can be reduced by using a combination of managed protection strategies, security applications and physical security systems.

> **Key Point**
>
> The strategies outlined here can be applied to any size system within a home, school or organisation.

Common Protection and Detection Methods

- **Penetration testing:**
  - is used to find potential vulnerabilities within a computer system that could be exploited for criminal purposes
  - is usually carried out by security specialists that offer their services to organisations with security concerns.
- **Anti-malware:**
  - is designed to spot a malicious virus, worm, Trojan, adware or spyware program and to remove it from a system or network
  - must be regularly updated to meet the latest threats that appear on a daily basis.
- **Firewalls:**
  - control the transmission of data between a computer and other network computers or the Internet
  - can be configured to apply rules to certain programs, websites or network connections
  - can be either software or hardware based – a hardware firewall is generally more expensive but more robust.
- **User access levels:**
  - are used to control the information that a specific user, or groups of users, can access, read or edit
  - may be limited to data that is relevant only to them or to protect personal information
  - are essential as users are often the weakest link in any computer system in respect to security.

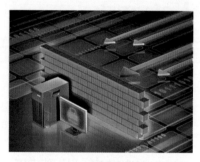

> **Key Point**
>
> Users failing to regularly update operating systems or anti-malware software is often the cause of computers becoming infected with a virus.

- **Passwords:**
  - are essential in preventing unauthorised access to a computer system, but they need to be complex enough so that they cannot be guessed or calculated by hackers.
- **Encryption:**
  - converts information using a **public encryption key** into a meaningless form that cannot be read if intercepted:
    - the only way to decrypt the information is with a **private key** or **cypher** generated by the owner
    - the encrypted text and the cypher are never transmitted together.
- **Physical security:**
  - is a practical way to protect equipment and data from external attackers
  - protects important network equipment or data by physically preventing access
  - may include the following:
    - the use of safes, locked rooms or obstacles to protect equipment
    - increased surveillance on equipment
    - removable hard drives or data storage that can be locked away from systems
    - biometric scanners that check fingerprints, iris or facial scans or voice recognition systems.

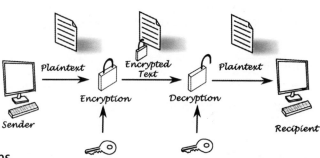

Plaintext → Encryption → Encrypted Text → Decryption → Plaintext

Sender   Public Key   Private Key   Recipient

What is a Strong Password?

- The security of any computer system, application or website is only as strong as the passwords used to access it.
- When creating a password, always follow these rules:
  - Make sure passwords are at least eight characters long.
  - Use upper- and lower-case characters.
  - Include special characters (for example ?, # and %).
  - Avoid real dictionary words.
  - Avoid any personal information – such as names of family members or pets, important dates or telephone numbers.
  - Regularly change passwords and never use them for more than one system.
- Password management software is a good way of creating and storing unique, complex passwords. They require a master password to access them.

Key Words

penetration testing
anti-malware
firewalls
user access levels
passwords
encryption
public encryption key
private key
cypher
physical security

> ### Quick Test
>
> 1. List three systems used at home that include encryption.
> 2. Why should a password never be used for more than one system?
> 3. Why might an organisation use a hacker to carry out penetration testing?

System Software

You must be able to:

- Describe the purpose and function of system software
- Explain the role of an operating system within a computer system
- Describe the various uses of utility and application software.

Why Do We Need an Operating System?

- The **operating system** (OS) is the link between the hardware, the software and the user, and it is essential to the function of any computer.
- The OS allows the user to access applications and allows the CPU to communicate with peripheral devices and system memory.
- All modern computer systems (for example smartphones, tablets, and portable and desktop computers) use an OS.

> **Key Point**
>
> No matter what size a modern computer is, it will have an OS.

> **Key Point**
>
> The most common operating systems today are Windows, Apple OS, Google Android and Linux.

Operating System Key Functions

- Modern OSs provide a **graphical user interface** (GUI) that allows ease of use without having to enter commands into a command line prompt. This includes the use of a mouse to select menus and objects and visual drag and drop file management.
- **Multitasking** is the process of carrying out multiple tasks simultaneously, working on a spreadsheet whilst listening to Internet radio for example. The OS will take advantage of multicore CPUs and **memory management**. By managing and allocating free space and prioritising the amount of memory and resources that the CPU and memory modules can use, non-essential processes can be slowed down and priority applications run simultaneously. The OS can also create **buffers** to allocate free memory to tasks that only require temporary storage of data, such as a printing a document.
- The OS will also manage **peripheral** devices such as printers, scanners, graphics tablets and webcams. Each will require specific software, or **drivers**, to communicate with the main

> **Key Point**
>
> The OS controls and manages the flow of data between the CPU and the other hardware devices in the system.

system and the OS will, where possible, automatically install and update these drivers as required.

- **User management** allows the creation and management of multiple user accounts to a system. Each user can be assigned individual:
  - access rights for both applications and files
  - security privileges in respect to what they can read, edit and delete.
- **File management** allows users to organise their work into folders and subfolders with appropriate filenames. Once organised, information can then be sorted and searched as required.
- Threat prevention is now a key element of all operating systems; regular security updates help prevent potential attacks.

Why is Utility Software Important?

- **Utility software** performs specialised tasks that support the OS.
- This may be included as part of the OS installation or may be additional **third-party applications**.
- Utility software functionality may relate to system security or to file and disk management.

What Tasks are Performed by Utility Software?

- Encryption software scrambles data into an unreadable form that cannot be read unless you have a specific key to decrypt it. This may be used to protect important documents containing financial or personal information.
- **Defragmentation** software analyses system data and how it is stored on the hard disk. It then rearranges the data into a more logical sequence to allow faster access on disks containing lots of data.
- **Compression** software reduces the file size of documents and system files so that they take up less space on a disk. Compression is often used when sending large files via email, or storing large multimedia files.

> **Key Point**
>
> Utility software usually runs in the background, performing maintenance tasks or 'housekeeping'.

> **Key Point**
>
> Third-party applications are not created by the operating system designers but written to run within it.

> **Key Words**
>
> operating system
> graphical user interface
> multitasking
> memory management
> buffers
> peripherals
> drivers
> user management
> file management
> utility software
> third-party applications
> defragmentation
> compression

> **Quick Test**
>
> 1. Find examples of four current operating systems.
> 2. Creating a presentation whilst listening to a podcast at the same time is an example of?
> 3. Look at the computer system you have access to. Can you list examples of utility software installed?

Wired and Wireless Networks 1

1 State **two** reasons why a smart TV would have network access. **[2]**

2 Name a network device used to share data between other devices. **[1]**

3 *A WAN can link a maximum of two LANs.* True or false? **[1]**

4 Describe what is meant by the term 'bandwidth'. **[1]**

5 Name **one** household kitchen device that can cause wireless network interference. **[1]**

6 Describe **two** benefits of the client–server network. **[2]**

7 Describe a potential benefit of connecting schools across the world using a WAN. **[1]**

8 A peer-to-peer network often shares security permissions. What does this mean? **[1]**

Wired and Wireless Networks 2

1. Complete the paragraph below using the words from the box. **[2]**

   | router   switch |

   A .... connects compatible devices together and allows data to be shared,

   creating a network. A .... connects different networks together.

2. *Modern computers often have an integrated NIC, meaning that an additional card is not required.*

   True or false? .... **[1]**

3. What device is often used to extend the range of a wireless network? **[1]**

   ....

4. What type of limited-range wireless connectivity is often used for computer peripherals such as speakers and controllers? **[1]**

   ....

5. In which decade did web pages first appear in the format we now recognise? **[1]**

   ....

6. What device is required to connect an existing LAN to the Internet? **[1]**

   ....

7. What is a main benefit of fibre-optic technology over traditional Ethernet cables? **[1]**

   ....

8. Describe **two** potential problems that a small business could face if it uses only cloud computing. **[2]**

   ....

   ....

9. How does the DNS system help users browse the Internet? **[1]**

   ....

Network Topologies

1 The sharing of network traffic between all devices is a benefit of which network topology? **[1]**

2 Name the topology that allows direct access between the server and each device. **[1]**

3 Which of the following would not normally be part of a network topology? Tick **one** box. **[1]**

A Laptop ☐

B Router ☐

C Server ☐

D Digital camera ☐

E Printer ☐

4 Match each topology with its potential problem. **[2]**

| Mesh | | If the server fails then the whole network will collapse. |
| Star | | Managing the network requires a high level of network expertise. |

5 State the device needed to connect one star network to another star network. **[1]**

Protocols and Layers

1 Which wireless system has a short range of around 10 m? [1]

2 What are common charging sockets across smartphone models an example of? [2]

3 What is the latest and most secure Wi-Fi encryption standard? [1]

4 In what format is a MAC address normally represented? [1]

5 192.168.1.2 is a typical .... [1]

6 Which email protocol is particularly suited to web-based email accounts? [1]

7 Which layer contains the HTTP, FTP and SMTP protocols? [1]

8 When purchasing devices to connect to a home wireless network, what identification mark should be looked for? [1]

9 State **two** common software standards. [2]

10 Describe the difference between a static IP address and a dynamic IP address. [2]

Common System Threats

1 List **three** pieces of personal information desired by online criminals. **[3]**

2 Complete the paragraph below using the words from the box. **[5]**

| hacker | social network | accounts | bank | password |

Using the same .... across systems, for example a .... and a ...., is dangerous. A .... gaining access to one will have access to many more of your ....

3 Malware is short for .... **[2]**

4 Which type of malware hides its true intention by pretending to be something else? **[1]**

5 A self-replicating form of malware is called a .... **[1]**

6 What is the purpose of ransomware? **[2]**

7 List **three** forms of social engineering. **[3]**

8   What is 'shouldering'?   **[2]**

9   How is blagging different from other social engineering methods?   **[1]**

10   How does a brute force attack work?   **[2]**

11   What does the abbreviation DoS stand for?   **[2]**

12   An important email is read by a hacker before it reaches its intended user. What is this known as?   **[1]**

Threat Prevention

1   Why must anti-malware be regularly updated?   **[1]**

2   Public and private keys are part of _____.   **[1]**

3   Hardware or software designed to control the transmission of data is called a

_____.   **[1]**

4 Match each term with its description. **[3]**

Physical security	Converts information into a meaningless form that cannot be read if intercepted
Encryption	Searching for potential weaknesses in a system that could be exploited
Penetration testing	A practical way to protect equipment and data from external attackers

5 Why might two users in the same network have different access levels? **[1]**

6 What is normally the weakest link in any network? **[1]**

7 Which **two** of the following should not form part of a password? Tick the correct boxes. **[2]**

A Upper-case and lower-case characters ☐

B Favourite pet names ☐

C Special characters ☐

D Telephone numbers ☐

System Software

1 An operating system is the link between which **three** elements? **[3]**

2 What is an area of free memory used to temporarily store information, such as a print file, called? **[1]**

3. List **four** examples of computer peripherals. [4]

_____

_____

_____

_____

4. Drag and drop became possible with which device? [1]

_____

5. If a device driver is not regularly updated, what may happen? [1]

_____

6. Complete the paragraph below using the words from the box. [3]

| system security | supports | management |

Utility software _____ the operating system, performing tasks such as

_____ and disk _____.

7. What is file compression? [1]

_____

_____

8. What is the rearranging of files to speed up access and reduce size called? [1]

_____

9. List **three** elements of user management. [3]

_____

_____

_____

Ethical and Legal Concerns

Quick Recall Quiz

You must be able to:

- Discuss the impacts of digital technoloogy on ethical and legal issues in our society
- Describe ethical concerns surrounding privacy, security and automation
- Describe legal issues arising as a result of increased use of computer technology.

Ethical Use

- The **ethical use** of computer technology means trying to cause no harm to others and acting in a morally responsible way to improve society.
- This applies to our own use of technology and to how others treat us.
- The anonimity and faceless nature of some systems, especially social networks, allows unethical choices to be made that might not be made in a face-to-face situation.

Are We Being Replaced?

- Robots and automated devices are ideal for situations that may be dangerous to humans or for jobs that are extremely repetitive:
  - Pilotless drones are now used routinely in military conflicts.
  - Robots are used to disable explosive devices and to enter environments poisonous to humans.
  - Manufacturing, from cars to games consoles, has been revolutionised by robots, carrying out repetitive tasks 24 hours a day, replicating the same movement exactly each time.
- But what happens to those individuals who are replaced? Is it ethical to replace people and not provide alternative employment? Could those people being replaced become manufacturing programmers?

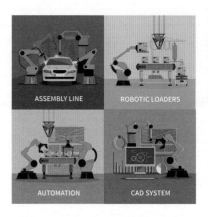

ASSEMBLY LINE   ROBOTIC LOADERS

AUTOMATION   CAD SYSTEM

Maintaining Our Privacy

- Our increased use of technology, smartphones, social networking and Internet-connected devices means that our actions are often recorded without us knowing it. Examples include:
  - Mobile phone service providers know our location through Global Positioning System (GPS) technology and mobile signal triangulation; they also know the people we contact and the mobile applications we use.
  - Websites track our search history using cookies and provide it to others.
  - Social networks routinely ask for personal information and like us to post it online.

GPS technology

Key Point

Cookies store personal information about your browsing history and login credentials.

- Internet service providers log our search histories, browsing data and file downloads.
- **Streaming services** log and analyse our music and video choices in order to make suggestions.

Privacy Concerns

- With so much data being gathered about our lives, many questions are being asked about how much of this information should be accessible.
  - Should mobile phones and Internet search records be routinely checked by government agencies for evidence of malicious intent, such as planning an act of terrorism?
  - What are social networks doing with our data and is our privacy worth free access to them?
  - Should our own access be restricted to prevent us accessing harmful information? Who should regulate this?
  - Is the **dark web** a reasonable alternative for those wanting online privacy?

New Opportunities for Crime

- The way that we interact with technology has increased our legal impact on society through online communication, and has created new opportunities for criminals.
- Criminals selling illegal products and services online, often using the dark web, have found customers around the world via the Internet (this kind of activity used to be limited to shady back-alley deals).
- Stolen personal information can be traded online and used to facilitate further crime.
- Government agencies struggle to keep up with the pace of computer crime.

Am I Breaking the Law?

- The vast amount of information available online also means that it is not always obvious when laws are broken. Users can quickly find films, music and games to download that break copyright laws.
- People can buy products from around the world, and have them delivered to their homes, without knowing the source of the product or whether it meets safety regulations.

Key Words

Global Positioning System
cookies
streaming services
dark web

Quick Test

1. Describe three ways that we share our private information online.
2. Describe three positive uses of drone technology.
3. What are the dangers of unregulated streaming services?

Cultural and Environmental Concerns

Quick Recall Quiz

You must be able to:

- Discuss the cultural impact of computer technology on our daily lives
- Describe the term 'digital divide' and how it came about
- Describe the environmental impact of computer technology on energy use and materials.

How our Lives are Changing

- Communication now includes text, picture and video messaging from any location in the world to another.
- We use social networks and **blogs** to publish our thoughts worldwide and we can contact directly on our smartphones the politicians and entertainment stars whom we read about!
- **Medical** advances include full-body scanners and smart watches that monitor our body and transmit the data online. Computer simulations analyse biological viruses and model new medicines.
- **Transport** technology is developing to automate not only the traffic lights and signals that we follow but also the vehicles that we use. Computer management systems control traditional motor vehicles, the latest electric-powered versions and the many driverless car prototypes now in production.
- **Educational** content now spans the world, and students who are able to get online can access not only local resources but also lessons delivered on almost any subject via video streaming services. The equipment used in classrooms also includes interactive whiteboards and **multimedia** systems.
- Many **leisure** activities, from **immersive** virtual reality gaming to three-dimensional cinema screens, use the latest computer-generated imagery (CGI). Streaming media services run complex algorithms to provide what they think we would like.
- The ability to not only find new jobs but also run an entire business online has completely changed the **employment** market.
- **Homeworking,** or remote working, is now possible using shared online platforms and video calling. The increased flexibility it brings is preferable to many families.

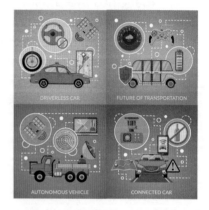

What is the Digital Divide?

- The **digital divide** is the social and economic gap between those who have and those who do not have access to computer technology.
- The increased access to technology is not consistent across the world or even within countries.
- Many countries/areas are limited by financial or geographical constraints, and broadband Internet connections are not yet available everywhere.

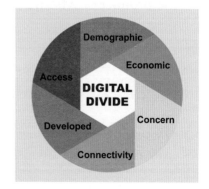

- This lack of access can then expand the divide further. For example:
  - Some jobs are advertised initially (or only) online.
  - Customers can usually find the cheapest products and household services through the Internet.
- The Covid-19 pandemic led to adults around the world working from home and children receiving lessons online. This highlighted the digital divide between those who had the technology and those who did not.

The Impact on the Environment

- Developments in computer science affect our environment in both positive and negative ways.

Positive	Negative
Reductions in the use of paper.	Increased energy consumption of digital devices.
Replacement of physical media with downloads reduces material costs.	Increased greenhouse gas emissions to meet additional power needs around the world.
Increased broadband connectivity allows homeworking and video calls, reducing the numbers of commuters and transport requirements.	Cost of the transportation of raw and synthetic materials for the production of smart devices.
Smarter devices control their energy usage to meet our needs – this reduces wastage.	It is difficult to recycle waste materials from outdated or unwanted technology.
The development of increasingly efficient renewable energy sources.	Devices often use rare earth elements that cannot be replaced and can be toxic to the environment when put in landfill.

 Quick Test

1. List three ways that recycling old computers can help the environment.
2. What are some of the concerns about driverless cars?
3. Research five rare elements currently used in the production of a smartphone.

Key Words

blogs
multimedia
immersive
homeworking
digital divide

Computer Science Legislation

You must be able to:

- Describe the reasons for and key concepts behind the following: the Data Protection Act 2018, the Computer Misuse Act 1990, the Copyright, Designs and Patents Act 1988
- Understand the difference between open source and proprietary software.

Laws

- New laws exist to regulate our increased use of computer technology and to make sure that individuals and organisations can be held responsible for any misuse.

Data Protection Act 2018

- Recently updated, this act controls how your personal information is used by organisations, businesses or the government. It is the UK's response to General Data Protection Regulation (GDPR) rules that apply to all European Union member states. Its main principles are:
  - Data should be used fairly, lawfully and transparently.
  - Data must be obtained and used only for specified purposes.
  - Data shall be adequate, relevant and not excessive.
  - Data should be accurate and kept up to date.
  - Data should not be kept for longer than necessary.
  - Data must be kept safe and secure.
  - Those organisations working with our data are accountable for all data protection and must produce evidence of their compliance.

Computer Misuse Act 1990

- Designed specifically to prevent hacking and the damage of computer systems by the following means:
  - intentional unauthorised access to programs or data that are not normally accessible
  - unauthorised access to material that could be used for further criminal activities
  - intentional damage to data or software using malware.

Copyright, Designs and Patents Act 1988

- Provides the creators of music, books, films and games with the right to control how their products are accessed and sold. This means that no one else has the right to copy or sell their work without permission.
- Using the Internet to access and download free copies of such **copyrighted** material is therefore illegal, as no money or credit will have passed to the original creator.

Key Point

Illegal websites offering free streaming of the latest movies are breaking the Copyright, Designs and Patents Act 1988. These sites also often contain malware and are run by criminal organisations.

Software Licences

- Depending on the specific needs of the user, there are many options when it comes to choosing new software and its associated licence. Price, operating system, familiarity and ease of use should be considered.
- **Open source** software is created to be shared openly online at no cost, with no limits on how it can be edited (**source code** freely available), copied or distributed.
    - Examples include Linux OS, GIMP (GNU Image Manipulation Programme) and Audacity audio editing software.
    - Developers can access and edit the source code and completely redesign the software.
    - As a free product, updates, support and user issues may be limited or slower than proprietary software.
    - Users can try out lots of different applications without thinking about the costs involved.
- **Proprietary** software is owned by the individual or company who created it.
    - Permission to use the software is usually purchased through a licence, and the software cannot be edited (source code not available) or shared.
    - Often known as 'off-the shelf' software, it has a specific purpose that cannot be changed.
    - Online licensing also allows the software creator to specify how many users, or devices, can use the software to prevent unauthorised sharing.
    - Users need to be aware that sometimes software is updated and a new licence needs to be purchased.
    - Telephone or online support is usually provided, but this may be time limited.

The Right Type of Software Licence

- When purchasing proprietary software, the following options should be considered:
    - Is it for one user or for a whole site (an office or school, for example)?
    - How many people will be using it concurrently (at the same time)?
    - Will the licence run for ever or will it need to be renewed monthly or annually as a subscription?
    - Does the software need to be linked to a specific computer (a 3D printing workstation, for example)?

Key Point

Many of us now use both free (open source) and purchased (proprietary) software.

Key Point

Just because a video game is free, it may not be open source. It may make money through advertising or in-game purchases.

Key Words

copyrighted
open source
source code
proprietary

Quick Test

1. Which Act was specifically designed to prosecute hackers?
2. When working from home with a limited budget, why might someone choose an open-source word processor?
3. Which act would apply when ensuring an organisation's customer records are kept up to date?

Common System Threats

1 Name **three** areas of our lives in which we are now often connected to networks. **[3]**

2 Your computer is infected with spyware. Describe **two** ways that the creator of the spyware may profit. **[2]**

3 What term describes the process of redirecting your browser to a fake version of a popular site? **[1]**

4 Deleting a user's document files or corrupting start-up files, preventing a computer from booting, is a possible symptom of a _____. **[1]**

5 What is the purpose of adware? **[2]**

6 Impersonating a friend or a financial organisation via a text message is an example of _____. **[1]**

7 Why do computer scams often target the young and the elderly? **[1]**

8 Apart from at an ATM, give **two** examples of where shouldering might take place. **[2]**

9 Name **three** types of valuable information that can be collected using data interception and theft. **[3]**

10 Give **two** examples of demands often made following a denial of service attack. [2]

11 What does the abbreviation SQL stand for? [3]

12 How does an SQL injection attack work? [3]

Threat Prevention

1 Name **three** pieces of malware that anti-malware is designed to stop. [3]

2 Which kind of firewall is more robust: hardware based or software based? [1]

3 Why do instant messaging systems use encryption? [2]

4 List **three** threat prevention strategies. [3]

5 Why might an online auction site use penetration testing? [2]

6 Why might a portable USB drive be a risk to a large network? [2]

7 User access level may be linked to read/write file access. Explain the difference between read and write. [2]

8 Describe a potential problem with a long complex password. [1]

9 Which **two** of the following would be classed as a strong password? Tick the correct options. [2]

A $thfL98&2hgf ☐   B P@55word ☐   C FFj32* ☐

D blue12345 ☐   E QWERTY2017 ☐   F iTYf76v()-@qPL ☐

10 Why should a password be changed regularly? [1]

11 Why are users told to avoid using dictionary words in passwords? [1]

System Software

1 Name **three** devices that use operating systems. [3]

2 List **three** current operating systems. [3]

3 Before modern user interface systems, what was the standard for user access? [1]

_____

4 Describe **two** key elements of a user interface system. [2]

_____

_____

5 What is OS user management? [1]

_____

6 How is user management beneficial? [2]

_____

_____

7 In relation to an OS, what is meant by third-party applications? [1]

_____

8 Why might a company use encryption software to encrypt its stored data? [1]

_____

9 List **three** types of file that can be compressed for easier email transmission. [3]

_____

_____

_____

10 A school computer is running slower than normal. Suggest a type of utility software that might help and how it works. [2]

_____

_____

11 Which of the following is a definition of utility software? Tick the correct option. [1]

   A Small programs used to run peripheral devices. ☐

   B Software used to write a letter. ☐

   C A first-person action game. ☐

Ethical and Legal Concerns

1 What does the abbreviation GPS stand for? [1]

2 What are cookies and what do they contain? [2]

3 Describe **three** Internet security and privacy concerns. [3]

4 Describe **two** benefits of robotic car manufacturing. [2]

5 Give **two** reasons why selling illegal products online is appealing to criminals. [2]

6 What laws do Internet users often break without realising? [1]

7 Identify **one** reason that government agencies access our online communications. [1]

8 How can access to a user's Internet history prevent cyberbullying? [1]

9 Identify **one** fun, **one** commercial and **one** government use for drones.   [3]

....

....

....

10 Why are hackers interested in our social network pages?   [2]

....

....

Cultural and Environmental Concerns

1 List **three** areas of our lives that are being changed by technology.   [3]

....

....

....

2 Identify **two** contributions to the digital divide.   [2]

....

....

3 Complete the following table by placing a tick in **one** of the columns for each impact to indicate if it is positive or negative for the environment.   [3]

Impact	Positive	Negative
Replacement of physical media with downloads.		
Cost of the transportation of raw and synthetic materials for the production of smart devices.		
The development of renewable energy sources.		

4 Describe **one** major benefit of online educational material.   [1]

....

5 Why are smartphones often difficult to recycle? [1]

6 Describe **one** potential benefit and **one** potential drawback of driverless cars. [2]

7 Define the term 'immersive gaming'. [1]

8 Why might a family's access to the Internet be limited by geographic constraints? [1]

9 Describe **two** benefits of moving towards a paperless office. [2]

Computer Science Legislation

1 State **three** principles of the Data Protection Act 2018. [3]

2 'Unauthorised access' and 'intentional damage' are common terms in which set of guidelines? [1]

3 Data should not be 'excessive'. What does this term mean in a legislative context? [1]

4   Websites that offer the latest cinema releases to stream for free are breaking which Act?   **[1]**

5   The Computer Misuse Act 1990 targets which particular computer crime?   **[1]**

6   *Open source software is owned by the company that created it and cannot be used without permission.* True or false?

     [1]

7   Which Act states that those processing our data are accountable for its protection?   **[1]**

8   What is a data subject, as referred to in the Data Protection Act 2018?   **[1]**

9   Intentional damage using malware is a crime according to which Act?   **[1]**

10   State **three** factors to consider when choosing a software application.   **[3]**

Algorithms and Flowcharts

You must be able to:

- Understand the term 'algorithm' and its relationship with computer science
- Explain the term 'computational thinking'
- Represent an algorithm using structure diagrams and flowcharts.

What is an Algorithm?

- To us and to a computer, an **algorithm** is a sequence of step-by-step instructions to solve a problem or carry out a task. Real-life examples might include:
  - getting ready for school
  - making a sandwich
  - setting up a bank account
  - starting up a games console
  - logging into a computer.

A sandwich algorithm could be written as:

1. Take two slices of bread from packet.
2. Take butter and filling from fridge.
3. Spread butter on bread with knife.
4. Add filling on top of one slice.
5. Place second slice on top.
6. Cut sandwich in two.
7. Eat sandwich!

What is Computational Thinking?

- The ability to solve problems in a structured, logical way is referred to as **computational thinking** and includes the following skills:

Abstraction	The removal of unwanted or unnecessary information from a task. This allows focus and clarity when solving problems.
Decomposition	The process of breaking tasks into smaller tasks that are easier to understand and then solve.
Algorithmic thinking	Being able to imagine a solution to a problem in a series of logical steps.

Analysing a Problem

- When looking at a problem, it is important to consider the essential inputs, processes and output before any coding takes place.
- This will allow a programmer to clearly define the system's purpose and functional requirements.
- This information can then be used to create structure diagrams that will lead to the generation of flowcharts and pseudocode.

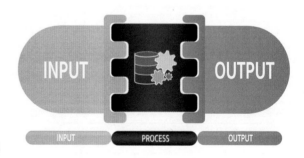

Input	include any data that will be entered into a system.
Processes	include any validation, calculations or operations carried out on a set of data.
Output	include any information that will be returned to the user.

What is a Structure Diagram?

- **Structure diagrams** are used to graphically represent a problem and break it down into smaller problems.
- This **top-level** approach allows individual elements to be tackled and eventually written as program and sub-program code.
- The top level represents the problem and each level below it is that problem broken down into one or more subsections. Ideally, each of the subsections will then relate to a sub-program with a specific task.

What is a Flowchart?

- **Flowcharts** are used to visualise an algorithm and show clearly the flow of information.
- They are generally used to plan computer programs before any coding is written.

Example of a Structure Diagram

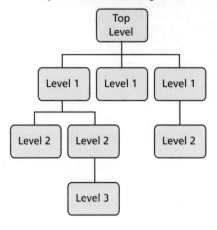

Standard Flowchart Symbols

(rounded rectangle)	Used at the start or end point of a flow diagram.
(parallelogram)	Used to represent the input or output of data in a process.
(diamond)	Used when a decision or choice must be made.
(rectangle)	A process symbol, used to indicate a process or computational task being carried out.
(rectangle with side bars)	Used to represent a sub-routine that can be called at various points of an algorithm.

An Example Flowchart

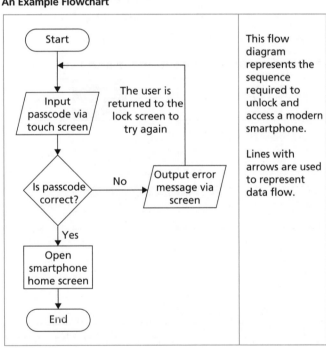

This flow diagram represents the sequence required to unlock and access a modern smartphone.

Lines with arrows are used to represent data flow.

Key Point

The flowchart shown will continue as an infinite loop until the correct passcode is entered.

Key Words

algorithm
computational thinking
abstraction
decomposition
algorithmic thinking
input
processes
output
structure diagram
flowchart

Quick Test

1. What does the 'top level' represent in a structure diagram?
2. What process would be used to simplify a task by removing irrelevant information?

Searching and Sorting Algorithms

Quick Recall Quiz

You must be able to:

- Describe standard searching algorithms
- Describe standard sorting algorithms.

Searching Algorithms

- Searching for information based on a given criterion is a common task for computer algorithms. Two common methods are binary search and linear search:

1. **Binary search** looks for a specific value in an ordered or sorted list by:
   - comparing it with the middle or median value and deciding if it is higher or lower
   - taking the half of the list that is higher or lower and once again finding and comparing it with the middle or median value
   - repeating this process until the specific value is found.

An example of a binary search: searching for 43 in this sequence

The middle or median number is 23.

1	3	6	12	23	43	51	66	80

43 is higher than 23, look to the right.

1	3	6	12	23	43	51	66	80

43 is lower than the median; look to the left.

1	3	6	12	23	43	51	66	80

43 is lower than 51; value has been found.

1	3	6	12	23	_43_	51	66	80

2. **Linear search** simply takes each value in a list, one at a time, and compares it with the value required. This is repeated until the correct value is found. This process can be very slow, especially with large data sets.

An example of a linear search: searching for 12 in the same sequence

1	3	6	12	23	43	51	66	80

1	3	6	12	23	43	51	66	80

1	3	6	12	23	43	51	66	80

1	3	6	_12_	23	43	51	66	80

Sorting Algorithms

- Sorting data means that data is generally easier to search, and it allows for more efficient algorithms. Three common methods are:

Bubble Sort	The first two values in a list are compared with each other and are swapped if they are in the wrong order. Then the next pair of values is checked and their order in the list is swapped, if required. This process is repeated until no further swaps are needed and the list is sorted.
Merge Sort	Data is repeatedly split into halves until each list contains only one item. The items are then merged back together into the order required.
Insertion Sort	Each item in an unordered list is examined in turn and compared with the previous items in the list. Higher values than those before them are left in the same position, but lower values are compared with each in turn until they can be inserted into the correct place. This process is repeated until all items have been examined and inserted into their correct position, in ascending order.

Bubble Sort
Sorting the sequence 3, 1, 6, 4, 8

First Pass:
(3 1 6 4 8) → (1 3 6 4 8) Swap 3 and 1
(1 3 6 4 8) → (1 3 6 4 8) 3 and 6 OK
(1 3 6 4 8) → (1 3 4 6 8) Swap 6 and 4
(1 3 4 6 8) → (1 3 4 6 8) 6 and 8 OK

Second Pass:
(1 3 4 6 8) → (1 3 4 6 8) 1 and 3 OK
(1 3 4 6 8) → (1 3 4 6 8) 3 and 4 OK
(1 3 4 6 8) → (1 3 4 6 8) 4 and 6 OK
(1 3 4 6 8) → (1 3 4 6 8) 6 and 8 OK
Completing a full pass without any swaps means the sort is now complete.

> **Key Point**
>
> Sorts can be carried out numerically or alphabetically

Insertion Sort

Look at each in turn	9	7	4	15	2	11
Move 7 to front	9	7	4	15	2	11
Move 4 to front	7	9	4	15	2	11
Leave 15	4	7	9	15	2	11
Move 2 to front	4	7	9	15	2	11
Move 11 before 15	2	4	7	9	15	11
	2	4	7	9	11	15

Merge Sort
An efficient sort for large data sets

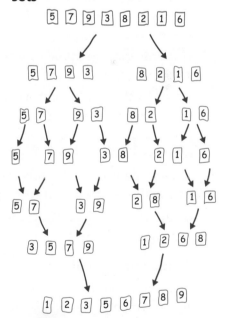

> **Key Words**
>
> binary search
> linear search
> bubble sort
> merge sort
> insertion sort

> **Quick Test**
>
> 1. Which type of search would be quickest with a large data set?
> 2. Which type of sort continuously compares each pair of values?

Pseudocode 1

You must be able to:

- Understand how pseudocode is used as a basic coding language
- Describe common pseudocode terms and keywords
- Write pseudocode to represent an algorithm.

Quick Recall Quiz

What is Pseudocode?

- **Pseudocode** is not a formal programming language. It is an informal way of describing computer instructions that programmers use to help plan a program before writing it in a specific language.
- Not designed to be understood directly by a computer, it uses terminology, syntax and structure common to most coding languages but in simple English.
- Simple mistakes that would halt a computer program, such as a bracket or quotation mark in the wrong place, will not have an impact on pseudocode.

Naming Conventions

- There are no fixed rules when it comes to naming variables or using keywords, but they must be consistent across multiple algorithms. The OCR examination board has created the **OCR Exam Reference Language**. This formally defined library provides students with examples of how pseudocode will be presented in the exam and students may be asked to respond to questions in this language.
- An example of naming a variable or constant is using a capital letter to show a second word. Spaces should not be used, for example firstName or highScore.

Variables and Constants

- A **variable** is part of a program that can be assigned a specific value. It consists of a descriptive **identifier** and the value assigned to it. A variable can be changed within a program as it runs and is not fixed. For example:

  heightTree = 125

- A **constant** is a value that cannot be changed or edited within a running program.
- A constant also has an identifier. For example:

  daysofWeek = 7

Comments

- Adding personal notes to coding helps others to understand it and helps to explain your own thinking.
- Comments do not affect the running of any program and may be denoted by //. For example:

  print("Hello, how can I help you?") // This line displays a welcome message

Common pseudocode keywords:

- **if** – used in a question, as part of a decision process
- **else** – used to provide a response if a statement is not met
- **then** – used to provide a response if a statement is met
- **while** – a loop with a condition set at the start
- **print** – used to display a response on screen to the user
- **input** – requires an entry from the user in response to a question
- **for** – used to create a counting loop.

> **Key Point**
>
> Remember that there are no fixed rules for pseudocode; it must just make sense so that it can be converted to a real programming language at a later date.

Please note that comments will be used in all of the following examples as guidance.

Input, Output and Print

- The input command requires the user to type in a response to a question that can be processed in some way. Displaying a message or returning a response to the user is referred to as an output. The print command is the most common way to display an output, using quotation marks. For example:

```
name = input("Please type your name") // Question requires input
print("Hello", name) // Displays a hello message followed by the name
just typed in
```

Sequence, Iteration and Selection

- **Sequence** is the act of carrying out a step-by-step process in a logical order.
- **Iteration** is the act of repeating any process until a specified result is reached. For example:

```
for i = 0 to 9
    print("Good Morning")
next i // Good Morning will be printed 10 times (0–9 inclusive)
```

- A while loop can be used to repeat a question until a specific answer is provided. For example:

```
while x = "python"
x = input("Name a language beginning with P")
do
    answer = input("Name a language beginning with P")
until answer == "Python" // Loop until Python is entered
```

- **Selection** allows decisions to be made within the program using if and else statements. Consider a true/false question for which the answer is false:

```
answer = input("Please answer True or False")
if answer == "True" then
    print("Sorry, incorrect answer")
elseif answer == "False" then
    print("Well done, correct answer") // Input is correct
else
    print("Answer not recognised") // Shown if anything else is entered
endif
```

Key Point

The symbols and operators used in these examples are explained on the next page.

Key Point

Refer to the OCR website or the specification to familiarise yourself with the OCR Exam Reference Language.

Key Words

pseudocode
variable
identifier
constant
sequence
iteration
selection

Quick Test

1. What is iteration?
2. Write down three possible constants in a program.

Pseudocode 2

Quick Recall Quiz

You must be able to:

- Understand the use of arithmetic operators
- Understand the use of Boolean operators
- Understand the use of comparison operators.

Common Errors in Algorithms

- The most common program errors are user-generated syntax errors, caused by entering incorrect code. A logic error is a fault in the design or structure of an algorithm.
- Program errors are covered in more detail on page 103.

Arithmetic Operators

- Mathematical calculations in pseudocode make use of the functions in this table. These operators may vary depending on the real programming language used when writing programs.

```
valueOne = 20
valueTwo = (valueOne + 10) / 6
valueThree = valueTwoMOD2
print(valueThree) // answer
should be 1
```

Operator	Function	Example
+	Addition of two or more values.	x = 10 + 5 x = 15
–	Subtraction of one value from another.	x = 20 – 10 x = 10
*	Multiplication of values.	x = 6 * 2 x = 12
/	One value divided by another.	x = 50 / 10 x = 5
MOD	**Modulus** – returns the remainder after a division.	x = 14MOD4 x = 2
DIV	**Quotient** – divides but returns only a whole number or integer.	x = 15DIV4 x = 3
^	**Exponentiation** – one value to the power of another.	x = 4^4 x = 256

Boolean Operators

- **Boolean operators**, or logical operators, are used in programs to define relationships, using Boolean logic, between data values.

Operator	Function	Example
AND	If two or more statements are true.	if 10>5 **AND** 5>2 (both are true)
OR	If either statement is true.	if 10==5 **OR** 10>5 (10>5 is true)
NOT	To reverse the logical results of a statement.	if **NOT**(5>10) (result is true)

> **Key Point**
>
> Note the differences between the OCR Exam Reference Language and real programming languages such as Python or JavaScript. You are allowed to use either in the exam.

Comparison Operators

- Comparison operators (or relational operators) are used by programmers to test the relationship between two values.
- They are essential in writing programs that include logic questions, user input or the analysis of numerical data.

Operator	Function
==	Exactly equal to
!=	Not equal to
<	Less than
<=	Less than or equal to
>	Greater than
>=	Greater than or equal to

```
pin = 9876
entry = input("Enter PIN")
if entry == pin
      print("PIN correct")
else
      print("PIN incorrect")
```

Trace Tables

A **trace table** is used to test an algorithm by examining each line of code step by step and predicting the results. It can be used to spot potential logic errors before code is written.

A Simple Looping Algorithm

LINE1: value = 3

LINE2: for i for 1 to 3

LINE3:   value = value * 2

LINE4:   print value

LINE5: next i

Line	Value	i	Output
1	3		
2		1	
3	6		
4			6
2		2	
3	12		
4			12
2		3	
3	24		
4			24

Key Point

Note the difference between a single =, used to assign a value, and a double ==, used in comparisons.

Key Point

A trace table will help spot logic errors but not syntax errors.

Key Words

syntax errors
logic errors
modulus
quotient
exponentiation
Boolean operators
comparison operators
trace table

Quick Test

1. Why are two equals signs used rather than one when using comparison operators?
2. If x = 20MOD6, what would be the result?
3. If NOT(3 == 3), would the result be true or false?

Boolean Logic

You must be able to:

- Explain the Boolean operators AND, OR and NOT
- Describe and create simple logic diagrams
- Represent logic diagrams using truth tables.

AND, OR and NOT

- Computer data is represented by a stream of binary data (0s and 1s).
- **Transistors** in a computer control the current flowing through it (off and on, 0 and 1), and the combination of multiple logic circuits using these two conditions allows more complex programs to be written.
- The Boolean operators AND, OR and NOT can be represented by **logic diagrams** or gates.
- Below each gate in the following diagram is a **truth table** representing potential inputs and outputs.

AND Gate

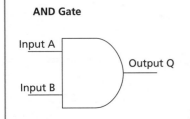

Inputs		Output
A	B	Q
0	0	0
1	0	0
0	1	0
1	1	1

OR Gate

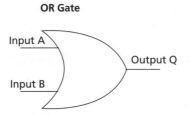

Inputs		Output
A	B	Q
0	0	0
1	0	1
0	1	1
1	1	1

NOT Gate

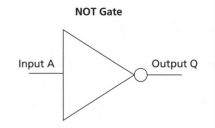

Inputs	Output
A	Q
0	1
1	0

Combining Logic Diagrams

- Adding together two or more gates allows more complex scenarios to be modelled. Consider the following scenarios:

Scenario 1:

Imagine a car on a fairground ride. On by default, a powerful lock P holds the car in place. It will not turn off, releasing the car, until the seat belt A AND the safety gate B are in place.

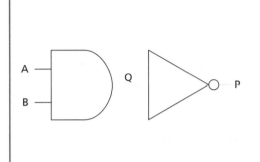

Inputs		Output	Output
A	B	Q	P
0	0	0	1
1	0	0	1
0	1	0	1
1	1	1	0

Scenario 2:

Imagine a security alarm circuit, which is set and running correctly when X is on. For this to happen, either of the alarm panels at B or C can be activated AND the door at A must be closed, deactivating a sensor.

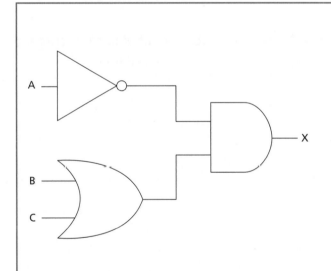

Inputs			Output
A	B	C	X
0	0	0	0
0	0	1	1
0	1	0	1
0	1	1	1
1	0	0	0
1	0	1	0
1	1	0	0
1	1	1	0

Quick Test

1. If a gate has two inputs and operates when either is on, which type of gate is it?
2. Which gate reverses the input signal?
3. How many potential inputs could a three-input gate have?

Key Words

transistors
logic diagrams
truth table

Ethical and Legal Concerns

1 Describe the term 'ethical use'. [2]

2 Mobile smartphone applications use GPS. Why is this? [1]

3 Why should we be concerned if an application asks for permission to access our contact details? [1]

4 State **one** positive and **one** negative impact on employment of the use of robots in manufacturing. [2]

5 Computer criminals are constantly experimenting with new ways to commit electronic crime. What problem does this cause for government agencies working to prevent crimes happening? [1]

6 Why do young people often break copyright laws online without realising? [2]

7 State **two** reasons why some people think that our Internet access should be filtered and controlled. [2]

Cultural and Environmental Concerns

1 Identify **one** positive and **one** negative aspect of online job applications. **[2]**

2 State **three** positive impacts on the environment of computer technology. **[3]**

3 Why are older members of society victims of the digital divide? **[1]**

4 What **two** factors will prevent a remote village from receiving the benefits of computer technology? **[2]**

5 What is e-waste? **[1]**

6 How can video streaming help teachers in rural areas? **[1]**

7 What piece of technology is often linked to immersive gaming? **[1]**

8 Why does the need for the 'latest gadget' have a negative impact on the environment? **[2]**

9 How might online communication improve a medical diagnosis? **[1]**

Computer Science Legislation

1 Match each issue with its related law. **[3]**

Two singers disagree over ownership of a song	Computer Misuse Act 1990
An employee takes a company's customer database to a new company	Copyright, Designs and Patent Act 1988
An online email server is hacked and personal messages are stolen	Data Protection Act 2018

2 Which Act incorporates European Union GDPR rules? **[1]**

3 What is the difference between open source software and proprietary software? **[2]**

4 List **four** types of copyright media that are often shared illegally online. **[4]**

5 In relation to data protection, what does the term 'transparent' mean? **[2]**

6 Trying to access computer programs or data that are not normally publicly available is a crime under which law? **[1]**

7 A family keeps receiving bills addressed to the previous owners of their home. Why should the Data Protection Act 2018 prevent this? **[2]**

8 A new business has found images online that it would like to use for its new website. What should it do to stay within the law? **[2]**

Where space is not provided, write your answers on a separate piece of paper.

Algorithms and Flowcharts

1 Define the term 'algorithm'. **[2]**

....

2 Match each term with its definition. **[3]**

Decomposition	Being able to imagine a solution to a problem in a series of logical steps.
Abstraction	The process of breaking tasks into smaller tasks that are easier to understand and then solve.
Algorithmic thinking	The removal of unwanted or unnecessary information from a task. This allows focus and clarity when solving problems.

3 What is the name of the information normally returned to the user? .... **[1]**

4 What shape is usually used to represent a decision in a flowchart? .... **[1]**

5 Provide a description of each of the following flowchart symbols. **[5]**

Shape					
Description					

Searching and Sorting Algorithms

1 Which of binary search and linear search is considered slower with large files, and why? **[2]**

....

2 Describe briefly how a bubble sort works. **[3]**

....

....

3 Name **two** other methods of sorting data in addition to the bubble sort. [2]

Pseudocode 1

1 State **two** reasons why pseudocode rather than a specific language is used to plan programs. [2]

2 Match each common pseudocode keyword with its definition. [7]

if	To display a response on screen to the user
else	To provide a response if a statement is not met
then	Requires an entry from the user in response to a question
while	To provide a response if a statement is met
print	Used in a question, as part of a decision process
input	Used to create a counting loop
for	A loop with a condition set at the start

3 Why is it important to be consistent with naming conventions in pseudocode? [1]

4 Complete the following table by placing a tick in **one** of the columns for each value to indicate whether it is a variable or a constant. [4]

Value	Variable	Constant
numberCars = 19		
daysofYear = 365		
hoursinDay = 24		
penWidth = 5		

5 Why are comments used in pseudocode? [1]

6 Write a simple algorithm in pseudocode that asks the user their favourite colour and then agrees with their choice, quoting the colour in the response. **[2]**

7 Write a simple program that keeps asking how many days there are in a week until the correct answer is given. **[4]**

Pseudocode 2

1 Define the following pseudocode comparison operators.

a) == .... **[1]**

b) != .... **[1]**

c) < .... **[1]**

d) <= .... **[1]**

e) > .... **[1]**

f) >= .... **[1]**

2 Which arithmetic operator returns the remainder after a division? .... **[1]**

3 What does the symbol '^' in 3^3 represent, and what would the answer be? **[2]**

....

4 Give **three** Boolean operators. **[3]**

....

5 How is the quotient function represented as an arithmetic operator? .... **[1]**

6 Find the value of x in the following statements.

a) x = 6 * 4 .... **[1]**

b) x = 3^6 .... **[1]**

c) x = 9DIV5 .... **[1]**

d) x = 21MOD10 .... **[1]**

7 Write a brief pseudocode program that asks what the temperature is outside. If the result falls between a value of 15 and a value of 25 then reply "Perfect!"; otherwise, reply "Not quite right". **[4]**

Boolean Logic

1 What electronic component can control the flow of electricity? **[1]**

....

2 Name the **three** types of gates shown in the following diagram. **[3]**

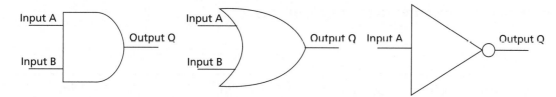

3 Complete the following OR gate truth table. **[4]**

Inputs		Output
A	**B**	**Q**
0	0	
1	0	
0	1	
1	1	

4 Create a logic diagram and truth table for each of the following scenarios.

a) A car (X) will not start until both doors (A AND B) and the boot (C) are closed. **[8]**

b) A water pump (X) will start if a water level sensor (A) deactivates OR if two switches (B AND C) are simultaneously pressed. **[8]**

5 Complete the truth table for the following logic diagram. **[8]**

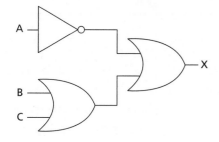

Inputs			Output
A	**B**	**C**	**X**

Quick Recall Quiz

Programming Techniques 1

You must be able to:

- Explain common programming data types
- Use basic string manipulation
- Use basic file-handling operations.

Data Types

- Categorising data allows a computer to treat each data type differently.

Data Type	Description	Examples	Pseudocode
Integer	A whole number with no decimal point.	4, 10, –20	int
Boolean	Digital data – can present only two values.	1/0, yes/no, true/false, on/off	bool
Real (or float)	All numbers, including those with a decimal point.	1.435, 0.01, –3.5	real (or float)
Character	A single letter, number or symbol.	T, £, @	char
String	A collection of alphanumeric data characters and symbols. Usually enclosed in quotation marks.	"Grace", "15-12-14", "Am@ze1"	str

- Casting, or typecasting, is the conversion of one data type into another, for example converting a string into an integer or a real number, or converting a number into a string:

```
int("17") // This converts the string 17 into an integer
str(125) // This converts a number into a string
```

> **Key Point**
>
> Real numbers are often referred to as floats and can be positive or negative numbers.

String Manipulation

- Normally written within quotation marks, a string is a collection of characters. Strings are often used in program inputs and outputs. For example:

```
string1 = "Press any key to continue"
print(string1) // This will print the above message on the screen
```

- Strings can be manipulated and handled in many ways. Consider the following string:

```
string1 = "Good morning"
print(string1) // This will simply print Good morning
print(string1.length) // This will print 12, the number of characters
including the space
print(string1.upper) // This will print GOOD MORNING in capitals
```

> **Key Point**
>
> Within a programming language such as Python, characters are simply a single character string rather than a separate data type.

- Substrings are created by selecting one or more characters from a string.

```
print(string1.[6]) // This will print the sixth character: o
print(string1(5, 7) // This will print seven characters, starting from
position 5 (position 0 being the first character G): morning
print(string1[-1]) // This will print the last character: g
```

- Concatenation is the joining of two or more strings. For example:

```
string1 = "Good morning"
string2 = " world!"
fullMessage = string1 + string2
print(fullMessage) // This will print Good morning world!
```

Key Point

The position of a character within a string starts at 0 from the left. A negative position can also be read from the right, starting with –1.

File Handling

- Programs often need to access external data in another file. They need to first open the file, then read the file, then write additional data if required and, finally, close the file.
- Consider an external text file of names called firstNames.txt
- A file handle called myFile will be a reference to the data:

```
myFile = openRead("firstNames.txt") // This will open the file in read-only mode
lineOne = myFile.readLine() // This will assign the first line as lineOne
lineTwo = myFile.readLine() // This will assign the second line as lineTwo
and so on
myFile.close() // This will close the file
```

Key Point

Reading a file does not edit the contents. Writing will create a new file or overwrite the contents of an existing file.

- Write mode enables a new file to be created or an existing file to be overwritten.
- To replace the list of names in the existing firstNames.txt file:

```
myFile = openWrite("firstNames.txt") // This will open the file in write mode
myFile.writeLine("Isobel") // This will replace the list with a single name
myFile.close() // This will close the file
```

- When reading a file with multiple entries, endOfFile() is used to determine when the end of the file is reached. For example:

```
myFile = openRead("firstNames.txt")
while NOT myFile.endOfFile() // A loop will run until the end of the file is reached
    print(myFile.readLine()) // Each line of the file is now printed
endwhile // The loop will continue until the end of the file is reached
myFile.close() // All entries having been printed, this will close the file
```

Key Words

integer
Boolean
real (or float)
character
string
alphanumeric
casting
substring
concatenation
write
overwrite

Quick Test

1. Which data type allows decimal places?
2. What term describes two strings joined together?
3. Which file-handling mode will replace the contents of a file?

Programming Techniques 2

You must be able to:

- Describe the use of records to store data
- Describe the use of SQL to search data.

Storing Records

- **Databases** are designed for storing large amounts of data, which can be categorised and structured for ease of accessibility.

memberID	userName	age	country	gamerRating
0001	ShonkiD	14	UK	5
0002	Sup3R1	42	USA	7
0003	ch@rlyB	25	UK	4.5

- Data is stored in tables containing **fields** (categories) and **records** (each row of related data).
- The **primary key** is a unique identifiable field that cannot be repeated.
- Imagine a games network user database called Gamers.
- Each field will have a specific data type.
- The primary key is memberID as each value within the field is unique.
- Three records are shown: 0001, 0002 and 0003.
- A **flat-file database** has only one table.
- A **relational database** has multiple databases, linked together by a field that is common to both databases.

Using Structured Query Language

- **Structured Query Language** (SQL) is a language designed to create, edit and search databases. Consider the games network user database already shown.
- The following examples use three key SQL commands:
  - SELECT: Used to fetch data from a specific column in a database.
  - FROM: Specifies the name of the database to retrieve information from.
  - WHERE: Used to limit the amount of data returned.
    - o To search for all usernames in the database:

```
SELECT userName FROM Gamers;
```

- o To search for a player for whom a condition is met (rating higher than 6):

```
SELECT userName FROM Gamers WHERE gamerRating > 6;
```

- o To search for a player from the UK:

```
SELECT userName FROM Gamers WHERE country = UK;
```

Random Number Generation

- There are often occasions when the creation of a random number is an important part of a computer program. This might be a lottery, encryption or 3D modelling system.
- Most high-level programming languages include a **random number generation** function that can return a value when called.
- An example represented in pseudocode might be:

```
lotteryNumber = random(1,59)
```

This would generate a random number between 1 and 59, including the start and end value.

Quick Test

1. What is a unique field with non-repeatable content called?
2. How many tables does a flat-file database normally contain?
3. Create an SQL search for a field called firstName from a database called addressBook.

Quick Recall Quiz

Programming Techniques 3

You must be able to:

- Use one-dimensional and two-dimensional arrays
- Effectively use sub-programs to help structure code.

Arrays

- An array is a data structure for storing related data of the same type within a program, meaning that several pieces of data can be stored under one name or variable.
- A **one-dimensional array** is a single list of common elements.
  - To create a string array with seven elements (the days of the week):

```
array week[7]
week[0] = "Sunday"
week[1] = "Monday"
week[2] = "Tueday" // Tuesday has been spelled incorrectly here on purpose
week[3] = "Wednesday"
week[4] = "Thursday"
week[5] = "Friday"
week[6] = "Saturday"
```

  - To print the days of the weekend:

```
print(week[6])
print(week[0])
```

  - To replace an element to correct a spelling:

```
week[2] = "Tuesday" // Completely replacing the element
```

  - Imagine a student with a range of five marks (out of 20) across a school term:

```
score = ["8","12","4","13","20"] // An array can also be created this way
```

  - A 'for' loop could be used to convert all values into a percentage:

```
for i = 0 to 4
    score[i] = score[i] / 20 * 100
next i
```

- A **two-dimensional array** can be represented as a table of rows and columns. Each position in the 2D array is referenced by numbers. So in the example shown on the right, testScore[1, 2] would be "9".

> **Key Point**
>
> Both one- and two-dimensional arrays must use the same data type.

	0	1	2
0	Liz	9	6
1	Gary	7	9
2	Rebecca	8	10

– To create this array:

```
testScore [2,2] // Declare the rows first and then the columns
testScore = [[Liz, "9","6"],[Gary, "7","9"],[Rebecca, "8","10"]]
```

– To search this array and output Rebecca's first grade:

```
testScore[2,1] // The resulting output would be 8
```

Sub-programs

- **Sub-programs**, or sub-routines, are used to save time and avoid repetitive code within the same program.
- Sub-programs can contain both **arguments** and **parameters**:
  - Parameters refer to variables passed to a sub-program.
  - Arguments refer to actual data used by a sub-program.
- The data from an array can be passed to a sub-program, processed and then returned.
- A **local variable**, or **constant**, is specified within a sub-program and can only be used within it.
- A **global variable**, or **constant**, can be referred to within the whole program, including sub-programs.
- There are two types of sub-program: **procedures** and **functions**.
- Procedures are a set of instructions that are grouped together and named to carry out a specific task.
  - A procedure for saying thank you when required:

```
procedure Thankyou(name)
    print("Thank you " + name) // The name variable will be set elsewhere
endprocedure
```

  - A procedure to count from 1 to 10:

```
procedure count()
    for x = 1 to 10
    next x
endprocedure
```

- Functions are similar to procedures but are designed to return a value that the program will use.
  - A function to generate the first number in a lottery system:

```
function lottery()
    number1 = random(1,59)
    return(number1)
endfunction
```

> **Key Point**
>
> A **fixed** or **static array** has a specific size or length that is set when created and cannot be changed.

> **Key Point**
>
> Variables and constants can be used in sub-programs in the same way as a linear-structured program.

> **Key Point**
>
> Most high-level programming languages distinguish between both types of sub-programs (procedures and functions). For example, in Python, both functions and procedures use "def()". The only way to spot the difference in Python is to look for the "return" statement.

> **Key Words**
>
> one-dimensional array
> two-dimensional array
> sub-programs
> arguments
> parameters
> local variable / constant
> global variable /
>   constant
> procedures
> functions

> **Quick Test**
>
> 1. Describe two benefits of sub-programs.
> 2. Which type of sub-program returns a value?

Producing Robust Programs

Quick Recall Quiz

You must be able to:

- Describe the term 'defensive design'
- Describe program maintainability
- Understand the importance of testing and using test data
- Describe how to spot program errors.

What is Defensive Design?

- It is important to consider all those who will be using a program and what level of access each user will be given.
- By **anticipating misuse** before it happens it can be defended against. This might include:
  - Users trying to access parts of the program they should not.
  - Users intentionally trying to break or crash a system.
  - Accidental misuse and key presses.
- **Authentication** is a means of checking the identity of the user. This might include:
  - Use of passwords to prevent unauthorised access.
  - Specific users can be given limited functionality.
  - Additional security question(s) can be asked.
- **Input validation** is making sure any user data entered is both accurate and in the correct data format. Checks might include:
  - Comparing against defined responses.
  - Allowing only specific data types.
  - Is the data entered outside of an expected range?

> ### Key Point
>
> Design programs to be accessed by users with good intentions and to anticipate users with bad intentions.

Program Maintainability

- A well-maintained program should be straightforward to access and edit by another programmer if at a later date it needs repairing or improving.
- Use the following to keep a program well maintained:

  - **Comments** – programmer notes to describe functionality (normally using # or // notation).
  - **Indentation** – this separates statements into groups and highlights features.
  - **Naming conventions** – ensuring variable names are sensible and purposeful, such as firstName or productCode.
  - **Sub-programs** – use these to avoid repetition and when they will benefit the program.

Why Do We Test Programs?

- It is essential that a program is tested fully before it is used. Effective testing checks all functionality and repairs potential errors before release.
  - **Iterative testing** is the cycle of design, development and testing. Test results enable redesign and redevelopment and the process repeats (iterates) until all elements are working.

    – **Final** (or **Terminal**) **testing** is carried out by real users when the program is complete and ready for release.

Spotting Program Errors

- Generating errors is a normal part of the program design process.

    – A **syntax error** is usually spotted by program compilers and interpreters and is specific to the programming language in use. Each language has its own formatting rules. A specific statement may have been typed incorrectly or an incorrect/invalid character may have been used.

    – A **logic error** is a fault in the structure or design of a program and more difficult to spot. Incorrect data types may have been used or lines of code may be out of place. Thorough testing is the only way to resolve logic errors.

Test Plans, Test Data and Refining Algorithms

- A **test plan** (or table) breaks down the program into a logical list of key functions and user pathways. Here is an example of a test table:

Test number	Test description	Expected result	Actual result	Action required
1	Welcome message	Hello message printed on screen	Message has incorrect spelling "Helo"	Edit print command "Hello"

- Suitable test data falls into the following categories:

    – **Normal data** (or **typical data**): Acceptable, error free data likely to be input into the program.
    – **Boundary data** (or **extreme data**): Correct data at the limit of what a program should be able to accept, minimum and maximum dates for example.
    – **Invalid data**: Data of the correct type but outside of predetermined limits that should be rejected, a username with too many characters for example.
    – **Erroneous data**: Data of the incorrect data type that should be rejected by the program or system.

- Using test data in **refining algorithms**, or programs, throughout their development improves efficiency and helps to remove errors.
- User testing is essential before any program is released to a larger audience. Users can pick up the problems and potential errors the programmer will miss. Fans of computer and console games often complain that games are released without thorough testing and often patches and updates are released after the public has played the game for a while.

> **Key Point**
>
> Syntax errors are human errors; for example, typing x instead of *. A logic error might be assuming every month in a calendar program has the same number of days; the program will run but incorrectly.

> **Key Words**
>
> anticipating misuse
> authentication
> input validation
> iterative testing
> final/terminal testing
> syntax error
> logic error
> test plan
> normal data
> boundary data
> invalid data
> erroneous data
> refining algorithms

Quick Test

1. Why should individual login details be added to programs that have multiple users?
2. Name two types of error specific to programming languages.

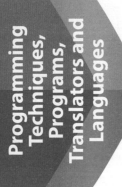
Languages, Translators and Integrated Development Environments

Quick Recall Quiz

You must be able to:

- Understand the need for high- and low-level programming languages
- Describe the purpose of translators
- Describe the characteristics of a compiler and an interpreter
- Describe the functionality of an integrated development environment.

The Need for Programming Languages

- Computers receive instructions from us through programming languages.
- Binary is the only language that computers understand, so whatever language we use must be translated into binary before it can be processed.

High-Level and Low-Level Languages

- **High-level languages** are written by humans and contain keywords and syntax that programmers understand.
  - Modern high-level languages include:

o **Python**	o **PHP**
o **The C family of languages**	o **Delphi**
o **Java / JavaScript**	o **BASIC**
o **Visual Basic / .Net**	

  - They share common terminology such as 'if', 'while' and 'until'.
- **Low-level languages** are more difficult to read and write, and they are much closer to direct instructions that a computer can understand. They are often used to directly control hardware.
  - **Machine code** is an example of a low-level language that can execute commands directly without any translation.

Translators

- Any programming language other than machine code must be translated into machine code before a computer can understand it.
- Modern **translators** include:
  - **Compilers** – used to read high-level languages and convert programs as a whole into machine code programs. Compilers will fail if errors are found, and the process must then begin again.

 Key Point

Machine code can be understood directly by a computer.

- Interpreters – used to examine a high-level language file one line at a time and convert each instruction into compatible machine code instructions. Although interpreters are slower than compilers, being able to translate while the program is running means that errors within specific lines of code can be identified more quickly.

Integrated Development Environment

- Modern integrated development environment (IDE) software allows programmers to design, develop and test their program ideas.
- Common functionality includes:
  - Editors – a text editor designed for writing source code. Tools to assist with formatting and syntax and the colour coding of statements help the programmer to spot errors.
  - Error diagnostics – also referred to as debugging tools, these will help to identify errors in particular lines of code.
  - Run-time environment – this allows programs to be run virtually within the IDE software, testing each line and allowing the programmer to spot and resolve errors.
  - Translators – these will compile or interpret the final code as required.

Key Point

There are a range of free and open source IDE applications for every programming language. Python IDLE is an example of a free IDE provided by the programming language creators.

Key Words

high-level languages
Python
C family
Java / JavaScript
Visual Basic / .Net
PHP
Delphi
BASIC
low-level languages
machine code
translators
compilers
interpreters
error diagnostics
run-time environment

Quick Test

1. Which low-level language can a computer understand without translation?
2. Which type of translator converts high-level language one line at a time while the program is running?
3. Name three high-level programming languages.

Where space is not provided, write your answers on a separate piece of paper.

Algorithms and Flowcharts

1 What is the ability to imagine a solution to a problem in a series of logical steps known as?

.... [1]

2 Complete the sentence using the words in the box below:

problem	top-down	structure

[3]

.... diagrams are used to graphically represent a ....

and break it down into smaller problems using a .... approach.

3 What is the purpose of the lines and arrows in an algorithm flowchart? [1]

....

4 Calling on a predefined sequence at different points of a flowchart would be an example

of using a .... [1]

5 Printing an on-screen message would normally be represented by which symbol? [1]

....

Searching and Sorting Algorithms

1 The number 14 in the following list cannot be searched for using a binary search. Why not? [1]

1 3 6 7 9 14 12

....

2 Describe briefly how a merge sort works. [3]

....

....

Pseudocode 1

1 Which common pseudocode keyword is used to create loops? **[1]**

2 Using a capital letter instead of a space to show a second word is an example of

.... **[1]**

3 What is the value named conversionFactor in the following code an example of?

```
costInPounds = costInPence / conversionFactor
```

[1]

4 What value should conversionFactor in the previous question be assigned? **[1]**

5 What part of the code below is a comment? **[1]**

```
print("Thank you and goodbye") // This closes the program
```

6 What does the following code do? **[3]**

```
quizAns = "B"
quizChoice = input("Enter A,B or C")
while quizChoice != "B"
    quizChoice = input("Try again")
endwhile
print("Correct answer")
```

Pseudocode 2

1 Fill in the missing word in the following sentence:

_____ operators are sometimes referred to as relational operators. **[1]**

2 Match each term with its definition. **[3]**

Boolean operators	Used to test the relationship between two values
Arithmetic operators	Used to define relationships using logical operators
Comparison operators	Used in mathematical calculations in pseudocode

3 Explain the difference between a single equals sign = and a double equals sign == with respect to operators. **[2]**

_____

_____

4 What operators are required to represent the following functions?

a) Less than. _____ **[1]**

b) Greater than. _____ **[1]**

c) Less than or equal to. _____ **[1]**

d) Greater than or equal to. _____ **[1]**

5 Which arithmetic operator returns the remainder after a division? **[1]**

_____

6 Which Boolean operator can be used to return a true response if either of two statements is true? **[1]**

_____

7 Complete the following sentence:

A _____ can be used to spot potential logic errors by examining each line of code step by step. **[1]**

Boolean Logic

1. Which logic gate is represented by a triangle? **[1]**

2. Complete the following AND gate truth table. **[4]**

Inputs		Output
A	**B**	**Q**
0	0	
1	0	
0	1	
1	1	

3. What do B, C and X represent in the following diagram? **[2]**

4. If an AND gate and a NOT gate are connected in series, what would be the output of the NOT gate if both inputs to the AND gate were turned off? **[1]**

5. If a binary logic diagram has four inputs, how many possible outputs are there? **[1]**

6. Which gate will give a true output if one or more of its inputs is high? **[1]**

7. Complete the following sentence.

    In a truth table, 0s and 1s are used to represent _____. **[2]**

Programming Techniques 1

1 Match each term with its definition. **[5]**

Integer	A single letter, number or symbol
Boolean	A whole number with no decimal point
Real (or float)	A collection of alphanumeric data characters and symbols
Character	Digital data – can present only two values
String	All numbers, including those with a decimal point

2 These are examples of which data type? 4.32, 0.3, –4.5 .... **[1]**

3 Define the term 'casting'. **[1]**

4 What would be the purpose of the following code? **[1]**

```
str(42)
```

5 Strings are normally contained within which symbols? .... **[1]**

6 What is the following code an example of? **[1]**

```
string1 = "Good Evening "
string2 = "Everyone."
fullMessage = string1 + string2
print(fullMessage)
```

7 Describe the difference between the two file-handling terms 'openRead' and 'openWrite'. **[2]**

8 Which code would normally be used to determine when the end of a multiple entry file is reached? **[1]**

9   What would be the function of the following code?   **[3]**

```
myFile = openWrite("petNames.txt")
myFile.writeLine("Poppy")
myFile.close()
```

Programming Techniques 2

1   Complete the following paragraph using the words from the box.

fields	primary key	data	records	tables

_____ is stored in _____ containing _____

(categories) and _____ (each row of related data). The _____

is a unique identifiable field that cannot be repeated.   **[5]**

2   Describe the difference between a flat-file database and a relational database.   **[2]**

3   What does the abbreviation SQL stand for? _____   **[1]**

4   Briefly describe the purpose of the following SQL command.   **[3]**

```
SELECT surnameName FROM Classlist WHERE examScore > 80
```

5   Write a statement in pseudocode that would
display a random number to represent a dice throw. _____   **[2]**

Programming Techniques 3

1   Define the term 'array'. _____   **[2]**

2   What type of array has rows and columns? _____   **[1]**

3   Variables within a sub-program (or sub-routine) are referred to as _____.   **[1]**

4   Name the **two** types of sub-program. _____   **[2]**

Producing Robust Programs

1. Name **four** defensive design considerations. [4]

2. Making sure any user data entered is both accurate and in the correct data format is known as? [1]

3. In addition to using comments, list **three** more program maintenance tips. [3]

4. What is the cycle of testing throughout the development of a program known as? [1]

5. Incorrectly typed functions and character-based mistakes in coding are usually described as which type of error? [1]

6. Match each term with its definition. [3]

Normal data	Values the program should not accept or process
Boundary data	Acceptable data likely to be input into the program
Erroneous data	Values at the limit of what a program can handle

7. Describe the need for a test plan when designing a program for commercial purposes. [2]

8. Give **five** headings that may form part of a test table. [5]

Languages, Translators and Integrated Development Environments

1 What is the difference between high-level programming languages and low-level programming languages? **[2]**

_____

_____

2 The only true language that a computer can understand is _____. **[1]**

3 Give an example of a low-level programming language. _____ **[1]**

4 Describe the purpose of a programming translator. **[2]**

_____

_____

5 Match each term with its description. **[3]**

Machine code	Used to read high-level languages and convert programs as a whole into machine code programs
Compilers	Examine high-level language files one line at a time and convert each instruction into compatible machine code instructions
Interpreters	An example of a low-level language that can execute commands directly without any translation

6 What does the abbreviation IDE stand for? _____ **[1]**

7 List **four** functions of a modern IDE. **[4]**

_____

_____

_____

_____

8 Colour coding scripts and highlighting syntax errors are features of which IDE function? **[1]**

_____

- During your course you will be given the opportunity to carry out one or more practical programming tasks. This will allow you to develop your programming skills and prepare you for the longer component 02 (section B) questions.

Choosing a High-Level Programming Language

Following briefs agreed with, or set by, your teacher, your work should be created using one of the following high-level languages:

- Python
- C Family of languages (C#, C++, etc.)
- Java
- JavaScript
- Visual Basic/.Net
- PHP
- Delphi
- BASIC.

Make sure to choose a high-level programming language from the list.

Programming Techniques

- The following practical programming skills are expected to be demonstrated:
  - the use of variables, operators, inputs, outputs and assignments
  - sequence, selection and iteration programming constructs
  - the use of count and condition controlled loops
  - multiple data types: Boolean, string, integer and real
  - basic string manipulation
  - file-handling operations: open, read, write and close
  - defining arrays
  - the use of functions and sub-programs to create well-structured code.

Project Analysis

- To create a practical programming solution, the brief or tasks should be broken down in a logical, structured way using computational thinking:
  - **Abstraction:** The removal of unwanted or unnecessary information from a task. This allows focus and clarity when solving problems.
  - **Decomposition:** The process of breaking tasks into smaller tasks that are easier to understand and then solve.
  - **Algorithmic thinking:** Being able to imagine a solution to a problem in a series of logical steps.

Practical Programming

Design, Write, Test and Refine

- You must be able to:
  - design a solution to the task
  - write code in a suitable high-level programming language
  - test your program appropriately
  - refine your program to improve its efficiency or remove errors.

Design	Write

• Based on the analysis of a brief, a detailed plan should include the following:
  – mind maps of ideas
  – flowcharts or diagrams
  – variables, input and output formats
  – data types
  – well-structured pseudocode with:
    o functions
    o sub-programs
    o comments explaining functionality and processing
  – the user experience and how they might navigate the program
  – consideration of suitable testing strategies.
	• Working from your design, you should be in a position to start writing and developing your code using a suitable high-level programming language. It should include:
	  – the use of comments to explain functionality
	  – sub-programs to improve efficiency
	  – the use of naming conventions
	  – a logical, modular structure that can be easily understood
	  – efficient use of built-in functions
	  – a practical user interface
	  – use of external data files in either text (.txt) or comma separated values (.csv) format.

Test	Refine

• Effective testing checks all functionality and repairs potential errors before external users have access to the program. You should include:
  – Iterative testing throughout the development of your code so that results are fed back into the development process.
  – Final, or terminal, testing when your code is complete.
  – A test plan that considers all aspects of the original task, along with your programming choices in respect to functionality.
  – Appropriate test data including:
    o normal, acceptable data
    o boundary data at the limit of what can be accepted
    o invalid data that cannot be processed
    o erroneous data of an incorrect data type.
	• As part of your practical programming skills, it is important that you are demonstrating the ability to refine your solution at all stages.
	• From early flowcharts to developed code, test and refine your algorithms to remove problems as they happen, not at the end of the project.
	• Invite potential end-users to try your program and give feedback. This can then be used to refine it.
	• Return to the brief. Are there now opportunities to improve your program to better meet its requirements?

Where space is not provided, write your answers on a separate piece of paper.

Programming Techniques 1

1 Give the pseudocode version of each of the following data types.

a) Integer .... [1]

b) Boolean .... [1]

c) Real .... [1]

d) Character .... [1]

e) String .... [1]

2 $, &, T and e are examples of which data type? .... [1]

3 The process of converting a string into an integer or converting a number into a string

is called .... [1]

4 Write a short program that defines the phrase "Good morning Dave" as string 1
and then prints the string. [2]

5 Adding two strings together to create a single string is called .... [1]

6 Consider the following string.

```
string1 = "Hello world!"
```

What would the following three lines of code print?

a)
```
print(string1.length)
```
....

b)
```
print(string1.upper)
```
....

c)
```
print(string1.[3])
```
.... [3]

7 What must always be considered when using the openWrite function with an existing file? [1]

....

Programming Techniques 2

1 In a database with the following fields, which field should be used as a primary key and why? **[2]**

identNumber	firstName	surname	postCode

2 To create a relational database, what must each table have? .... **[1]**

3 Briefly describe the purpose of SQL. **[2]**

4 Within an SQL database, what is the purpose of the command WHERE? **[1]**

Programming Techniques 3

1 Using code, create an array of the four seasons. **[2]**

2 Alternatively, an array can be defined in one line. Write an example line of code to specify a range of four different temperatures in the 20s. **[3]**

3 Based on the following table, called Survey, write a two-line piece of code that would create a two-dimensional array. **[4]**

7	6	9
7	4	3
7	6	6

4 What would the following search return? **[1]**

```
carSurvey[0,2]
```

5 Describe a key difference between a sub-program procedure and a sub-program function. **[2]**

Producing Robust Programs

1 Creating access-limited usernames and passwords and planning for user error are examples of _____. **[1]**

2 Using sub-programs and using user-friendly comments in coding are examples of

_____. **[1]**

3 Who should a programmer plan for? Tick the correct answer. **[1]**

A Experienced computer users. ☐

B Users who will make mistakes. ☐

C Users who try to break the program. ☐

D All of the above. ☐

4 Which of the following would be a poorly named variable and why? Tick the correct box and answer on the line underneath. **[2]**

A lastName ☐   **B** emailAddress ☐   **C** dataStuff ☐

_____

5 What is the name of the testing carried out on a program when it is complete? **[1]**

_____

6 An incorrectly spelt function or a misplaced character will normally return which type of error when a program is run? **[1]**

_____

7 Consider a program that asks for the month of the year in numerical format. Provide examples for the following test data categories.

a) Normal data _____ **[1]**

b) Boundary data _____ **[1]**

c) Erroneous data _____ **[1]**

8 What is the difference between an expected outcome and the actual outcome in a standard test table? **[2]**

Languages, Translators and Integrated Development Environments

1 Why are low-level languages more difficult to read and write than high-level languages? **[1]**

2 Briefly describe the purpose of a compiler. **[1]**

3 Why must a compiler restart any conversion if an error is found? **[1]**

4 Which type of translator translates a whole high-level program into a machine code program? **[1]**

5 When programming manufacturing equipment, what would be a major benefit of using an IDE? **[2]**

6 Which function of an IDE allows for virtual program testing? **[1]**

Mixed Questions

1. Richard decides to use an IDE (Integrated Development Environment) to create a new game.

   Identify **two** features of the IDE that Richard might use. [2]

2. Add together the following 8-bit binary numbers and show your answer in 8-bit and denary form. [3]

   00101010

   01000111

3. Why might the touch screen of a smartphone be described as an input and an output device? [2]

4. A newspaper office's computer has been attacked by a virus, and the newspaper's owners have been told that the virus is a form of ransomware.

   What does the term 'ransomware' mean? [2]

5. Many people still use the terms 'World Wide Web' and 'the Internet' to mean the same thing.

   Explain the difference between these terms. [2]

6 Write a short program using pseudocode that asks the user for their first and last name, and then uses concatenation to print both names on screen as the user's full name. **[3]**

7 Following the numbers 0–9, why are letters then used in the hexadecimal system? **[1]**

8 Helen has written a puzzle game using a high-level programming language. She can use either a compiler or an interpreter to translate the code.

Describe the differences between these methods. **[2]**

9 An estate agent is setting up a new office with a new network.

Describe **three** ways in which the information stored on computers can be kept secure. **[3]**

10 A social network web page has a feature that allows users to upload a photo. To prevent the server from being filled too quickly, a 1-MB limit needs to be applied.

Write a pseudocode sub-program that would do this. **[6]**

11 Why are software standards important when designing or updating an operating system? **[2]**

12 A lead designer in a programming team wants to make sure that the code they write can be easily followed by their team members at a later date.

Describe **four** ways of achieving this. **[4]**

13 Place the following units in order, from smallest to largest. **[1]**

GB   **bit**   **PB**   **byte**   **nibble**   **MB**

14 A young family is setting up the wireless network in their new home. They have options for **four** different encryption standards.

Name them, and explain which one the family should use and why. **[3]**

....

....

....

15 Rachel is buying secondary storage to back up her family photos.

State **four** characteristics of secondary storage she should consider when shopping. **[4]**

....

....

....

....

16 Explain the difference between a database field and a record. **[2]**

....

....

17 A desktop computer is running at full capacity and needs to create 'virtual memory' to try to help the machine to run more smoothly.

Explain the term 'virtual memory'. **[2]**

....

....

18 Isha is coding an art website. Visitors will be able to look at, and buy, her original artwork.

Provide two defensive design considerations and explain the role of each. **[4]**

19 The owners of a large clothing store have chosen a star topology for their LAN.

Provide **four** possible reasons why they have done this. **[4]**

20 Carry out a merge sort on the following numbers.   57, 32, 4, 5, 40, 54, 2 **[2]**

21 Daniel's new coffee maker contains an embedded system.

What is meant by the term 'embedded system'? **[2]**

22 Explain the difference between a single equals sign and a double equals sign when writing pseudocode. **[2]**

23 A school is considering moving the storage of student document folders to a cloud-based system.

Describe **two** advantages of doing this. **[4]**

24 As programmers started to collaborate all around the world, explain why the Unicode character set had to be created. **[2]**

25 A musical keyboard program uses a sub-program for each musical note.

Explain **two** benefits of using sub-programs. **[2]**

26 *Decimal, base 10 and denary are all counting systems based on the digits 0 and 1.*

True or false? **[1]**

27 Lee has been told to look for the HTTPS symbol when shopping online for a new mountain bike.

Why is this a good idea? **[2]**

28 A library customer database has the following fields.

memberID	surname	firstName	houseNo	postCode

a) Identify a suitable field to use as a primary key. .... **[1]**

b) Why does the database need a primary key? **[1]**

29 Explain the difference between volatile and non-volatile memory, and provide an example of each. **[4]**

30 Carry out a bubble sort on the following numbers.   **14, 22, 12, 18** **[2]**

31 A software programmer is starting to design a new word processor. She has been given a large list of requirements and design features to include.

Explain how abstraction will help the designer make a start. **[2]**

32 List **three** modern household devices that may contain an embedded system. **[3]**

33 Annie, a university student, has been introduced to a new peer-to-peer network by a friend.

What concerns might she have about using it? **[3]**

34 A bank account program requires users to enter their date of birth in the format DD/MM/YYYY.

State examples of normal, boundary and erroneous data. **[3]**

35 *Open source software is usually purchased through a licence, and the software cannot be edited or shared in any way.*

True or false? **[1]**

36 Keeping up with the latest gadgets and smartphones means that our devices are replaced regularly and are designed with a short lifespan.

What impact does this have on the environment? **[4]**

Mixed Questions

37 A community centre is delivering a talk to members on the dangers of social engineering.

Describe **three** methods the members should be made aware of. [3]

....

....

....

38 A graphic designer's computer is slowing down, and her friend has recommended defragmenting the hard drive.

Describe why this might help. [3]

....

....

....

39 A politician with controversial views has had his website closed by a denial of service attack.

Explain this method of network threat. [2]

....

....

40 *Portable hard drives and optical discs have fixed storage capacities.*

True or false? .... [1]

41 The number 181 can be represented in 8-bit binary.

.... 1 0 1 1 0 1 0 1 .... | LSM | | MSB |

a) What do the letters LSB and MSB stand for? [2]

....

....

b) Add the labels LSB and MSB to the left and right of the sequence above. [1]

42 Describe the difference between a Domain Name Service and Domain Name Servers. **[1]**

43 A programmer is working on a sub-program as part of a larger project; she is including local variables and global variables.

Describe the difference between these **two** types of variable. **[2]**

44 A new calendar application is being developed. State two examples of constants that might be included in its development. **[2]**

Answers

Pages 6–21 Revise Questions

Pages 6–7
1. The ALU
2. Registers either store memory locations or the actual data to be processed
3. Any four of the following: keyboard; microphone; mouse; webcam; sensor; drawing tablet; scanner

Pages 8–9
1. GHz
2. Each core is an individual CPU; tasks can be carried out simultaneously
3. a) Microwave, oven, mixer; program cycles, speed, timing and temperature controls
   b) Smart TV, games console, smart speakers; installable apps, voice control, disc drive controls

Pages 10–11
1. RAM
2. Usually because the installed RAM is full
3. ROM

Pages 12–13
1. They are cheap to manufacture and reproduce; the size and shape is child friendly to handle and load; they are easy to package and are portable
2. It has complex moving parts that will fail if the device is knocked or dropped
3. Examples: smartphones/tablets; lightweight laptops; digital/video cameras; USB storage devices; games consoles; high-end desktop computers

Pages 14–15
1. 4
2. To create an 8-bit (1-byte) character set
3. 256

Pages 16–17
1. 11000100
2. Any binary value greater than 255
3. 2

Pages 18–19
1. 35
2. 314
3. 2

Pages 20–21
1. 2.2 MB
2. Any suitable example, e.g. MP3
3. Lossless compression, to preserve the original file so no quality is lost

Pages 22–29 Practice Questions
Systems Architecture, Memory and Storage

The Purpose and Function of the Central Processing Unit
1. The brain [1]

2. [6]

Device	Input	Output
Keyboard	✓	
Printer		✓
Monitor		✓
Webcam	✓	
Sensor	✓	
Speakers		✓

3. The ALU [1]
4. The cache [1]
5. This controls the flow of data around the system [1]
6. This means that both the computer program [1] and the data it processes are stored in memory [1]
7. Memory Address Register [1] and Memory Data Register [1]
8. Accumulator [1]
9. The program counter [1]
10. The 1940s [1]

Systems Architecture
1. Fetch – The instruction is brought from memory
   Decode – The instruction is decoded to enable it to be understood
   Execute – The instruction is carried out [3]
2. GHz [1]
3. 4 [1]
4. The L1 cache [1]
5. Two billion [1]
6. Being able to carry out more than one task at the same time [1]
7. Any three of the following: DVD player [1]; washing machine [1]; dishwasher [1]; home cinema system [1]; microwave [1] (or similar)
8. Examples:
   a) Wi-Fi connectivity [1]; backlighting [1]; speaker control [1]; Internet browsing [1]
   b) Program control [1]; temperature sensor [1]; door lock control [1]

Memory
1. Random access memory [1] and read-only memory [1]
2. RAM [1]
3. ROM [1]
4. Once power is switched off [1] all data stored on volatile memory is lost [1]
5. RAM [1]
6. True [1]
7. Basic input/output system [1]
8. B [1]
9. If the RAM becomes full [1]
10. Because hard drive access is normally slower than access to RAM [1]
11. True [1]

Storage Types, Devices and Characteristics
1. So that programs do not have to be installed each time that we want to use them [1]
2. Magnetically [1]; optically [1]; SSD storage [1]
3. GB [1]
4. True [1]
5. KB, MB, GB, TB [1]
6. Capacity [1]; read/write speed [1]; portability [1]; durability [1]; reliability [1]; cost [1]
7. DVD [1]
8. SSD (flash) storage [1]
9. Any two of the following: fast read/write access [1]; no moving parts [1]; small size [1]
10. The lifespan of the device or method [1] and advances in storage technology [1]
11. Magnetic storage [1]

Units and Formats of Data
1. B [1]
2. 32 bits [1]
3. 6 GB [1]
4. Designed to convert alphanumeric characters [1] typed into a computer into a usable binary equivalent [1]
5. American Standard Code for Information Interchange [1]
6. 128 [1]
7. The original ASCII binary equivalent was a 7-bit code with 128 possible characters [1]; an extra bit was added to every binary sequence to create an 8-bit (1-byte) character set [1]
8. Unicode [1]

Converting Data 1
1. a) Base 10 [1]
   b) Base 2 [1]
2. a) 1 [1]
   b) 255 [1]
   c) 181 [1]
   d) 51 [1]
   e) 85 [1]
   f) 240 [1]
3. 11101000 [1]
4. 11111111 [1] because all 8 bits have been used [1]
5. An error caused by any binary value greater than 255 or 11111111 [1]
6. a) Multiply by 2 [1]
   b) Divide by 2 [1]

Converting Data 2
1. 0, 1, 2, 3, 4, 5, 6, 7, 8, 9, A, B, C, D, E, F [1]
2. To enable them to express large binary numbers more easily [1]
3. To prevent the duplication of numbers [1]
4. a) 31 [1]
   b) AD [1]
   c) 7E [1]
   d) E1 [1]
5. a) 109 [1]
   b) 59 [1]
   c) 117 [1]
6. 4 bits [1]

Audio/Visual Formats and Compression

1. Metadata – Additional information saved within the image file
   Colour depth – The number of bits per pixel
   Resolution – The number of pixels per inch used to create an image **[3]**
2. 00 **[1]**; 01 **[1]**; 10 **[1]**; 11 **[1]**
3. 1,000,500 pixels **[1]**
4. 15,876 MB **[1]**
5. A higher sample rate means that more bits are used to encode the sample, which will increase the file size **[1]**
6. Original fine detail can be lost if compression settings are too high **[1]**
7. Any three of the following: JPEG **[1]**; MP3 **[1]**; GIF **[1]**; MP4 **[1]**
8. True **[1]**

Pages 30–37 **Revise Questions**

Pages 30–31
1. To connect LANs in different banks around the world
2. The spread of viruses disguised as legitimate software or media; users not realising that their files are being shared
3. Quality of transmission media; interference from external sources; a large number of users on the same network

Pages 32–33
1. A router
2. The Domain Name Server or Service (DNS)
3. Sharing files; collaborative working; accessing remote files; playing multiplayer games; using online or browser-based software

Pages 34–35
1. Each device in the network is connected to every other device in the network
2. The network will fail
3. Any four of the following: router, switch, hub, desktop or laptop computer, network printer, tablet, smartphone

Pages 36–37
1. It allows different manufacturers to create network-compatible devices
2. IMAP

Pages 38–45 **Review Questions**
Systems Architecture, Memory and Storage

The Purpose and Function of the Central Processing Unit
1. Input **[1]**; process **[1]**; output **[1]**
2. Output **[1]**
3. The cache **[1]**
4. Arithmetic logic unit **[1]**
5. The control unit **[1]**
6. The bus **[1]**
7. MAR stores the location whilst the MDR stores the actual data **[1]**
8. An instruction or piece of data fetched from memory is stored in the MDR temporarily until used **[1]**
9. The ALU **[1]**

10. The MAR **[1]**

Systems Architecture
1. Execute **[1]**
2. True **[1]**
3. Decoded **[1]**
4. The L1 cache **[1]**; very fast **[1]**; slower **[1]**; more efficient **[1]**
5. True **[1]**
6. Clock speed **[1]**; cache size **[1]**; number of cores **[1]**
7. a) 6 **[1]**
   b) 4 **[1]**
   c) 1 **[1]**
   d) 2 **[1]**
   e) 8 **[1]**
8. A computer system with a specific function **[1]** within a larger system **[1]**

Memory
1. B **[1]**
2. ROM **[1]**
3. Data written to it is stored permanently **[1]**
4. RAM is much quicker to access **[1]**; the CPU can quickly identify memory locations in RAM **[1]**
5. ROM **[1]**
6. RAM **[1]**
7. The system hard drive **[1]**
8. RAM **[1]**; ROM **[1]**; CPU Cache **[1]**
9. User expandable memory is cheaper than factory-installed storage **[1]**; customers can specify their own storage requirements **[1]**

Storage Types, Devices and Characteristics
1. CPU **[1]**; motherboard **[1]**
2. Solid-state drive **[1]**
3. 8 **[1]**
4. 1,000,000 **[1]**
5. kilo – thousand
   mega – million
   giga – billion
   tera – trillion **[4]**
6. Blu-ray **[1]**
7. Magnetic storage **[1]**
8. Advantages (any two of the following): cheap **[1]**; portable **[1]**; widely available **[1]**. Disadvantages (any two of the following): easily damaged **[1]**; limited capacity **[1]**; correct player needed **[1]**
9. CD **[1]**; DVD **[1]**; Blu-ray **[1]**
10. Data can be transferred to and from the SSD more quickly **[1]**
11. When using such a device while walking or running, the complex drive would eventually become damaged **[1]**

Units and Formats of Data
1. Around 1 GB (music = 900 MB) **[1]**
2. C **[1]**
3. True **[1]**
4. 01111000 **[1]**; y **[1]**; 122 **[1]**
5. Unicode was developed as a world industry standard **[1]** to represent all known languages **[1]**
6. ASCII character/coding groups **[1]**

Converting Data 1
1. Decimal **[1]**
2. 1, 2, 4, 8, 16, 32, 64, 128 **[1]**
3. a) 00111100 **[1]**
   b) 10111101 **[1]**
   c) 00101000 **[1]**
   d) 00001011 **[1]**
   e) Overflow **[1]**
   f) 01100011 **[1]**
4. 2 **[1]**
5. 11010000 **[1]**; 26 **[1]** and 208 **[1]**
6. Because the value 0 is included **[1]**

Converting Data 2
1. 16 **[1]**
2. 2 **[1]**
3. a) 10001011 **[1]**
   b) 00010001 **[1]**
   c) 00111111 **[1]**
   d) 11110010 **[1]**
4. 2 **[1]**
5. False **[1]**
6. a) C7 **[1]**
   b) 32 **[1]**
   c) F2 **[1]**

Audio/Visual Formats and Compression
1. Pixels **[1]**
2.

0	0	1	1	0	0
0	1	1	1	1	0
1	1	1	1	1	1
1	1	1	1	1	1
0	1	0	0	1	0
1	0	0	1	0	0

[2]

3. Any three of the following: GPS data **[1]**; camera aperture and shutter speed **[1]**; date and time that a photograph was taken **[1]**; data added by the user **[1]**
4. 256 **[1]**
5. 0.48 MB **[3]**
6. Sampling **[1]**
7. The number of samples taken each second when converting into audio **[1]**
8. Less storage space required **[1]**; faster uploading and downloading **[1]**; online streaming services run more smoothly **[1]**
9. In lossless compression the original quality of files is preserved **[1]** when they are edited and resaved **[1]**

Pages 46–49 **Practice Questions**
Computer Networking

Wired and Wireless Networks 1
1. Any five of the following: laptop **[1]**; smartphone **[1]**; desktop **[1]**; smart TV **[1]**; router **[1]**; tablet **[1]**
2. Local area network **[1]**; wide area network **[1]**
3. The Internet **[1]**
4. Bandwidth **[1]**; external interference **[1]**; the number of users **[1]**
5. Multiple client computers **[1]** access a main computer server that controls access to the files and the data it stores **[1]**. This allows the central server to control security, user access and backups **[1]**.

6. Peer-to-peer network [1]
7. Bits per second [1]
8. Any of the following: users may not be aware that other users on the network can access their files [1]; malware can be spread between computers [1]; users are unaware of other users' locations [1]
9. Fibre-optic technology [1]

Wired and Wireless Networks 2
1. Network interface controller/card [1]
2. Wi-Fi [1]; Bluetooth [1]; 3G/4G mobile network [1]
3. Router [1]
4. Media access control [1]
5. Domain Name Service [1]
6. Internet Protocol [1]
7. Cloud computing [1]; Internet [1]; remote [1]; applications [1]
8. HTML [1]
9. The web-hosting company rents out web space on its Internet-connected server [1] and customers can then upload their web pages, making them accessible online all over the world. [1] Other companies are responsible for storing the data so customers must be able to trust them [1]

Network Topologies
1. Star [1]; mesh [1]
2. Server [1]
3. Advantages (any two of the following): the failure of one device, as long as it is not the server, will not affect the rest of the network [1]; additional devices can easily be added [1]; problems can be found easily [1]; data is quickly directed to a specific address by the server [1]. Disadvantages: if the server fails, so will the network [1]; extensive cabling and knowledge are required [1]
4. False [1]
5. Mesh topology [1]
6. Because each device is connected to every other device [1]
7. A device at an intersection/connection point within a network [1]

Protocols and Layers
1. Encryption prevents unauthorised access [1] and users accessing private information [1]
2. It is out of date [1]; it can be easily hacked [1]
3. Any three of the following: TCP/IP [1]; HTTP [1]; HTTPS [1]; FTP [1]; POP [1]; IMAP [1]; SMTP [1]
4. Layers [1]
5. HTTPS [1]
6. FTP [1]
7. Application layer – Data relevant to web browsers and email clients
   Transport layer – Ensures that data is correctly sent and received between network hosts
   Internet (or network) layer – Communicates the IP addresses of devices between routers
   Data link layer – Concerned with physical data transfer over cables [4]
8. Ethernet cable [1]
9. Transmission Control Protocol/Internet Protocol [1]

Pages 50–55 Revise Questions

Pages 50–51
1. Any five of the following: virus; worm; Trojan; spyware; adware; ransomware; pharming
2. The technique of watching a user at an ATM (or similar) and recording their PIN details
3. Keep one hand over the other as you type to shield your PIN details; keep your body close to the ATM machine, blocking the keyboard from view
4. Denial of service attack

Pages 52–53
1. Digital telephones; Wi-Fi networking; streaming music and video services; email services
2. If hackers acquire the password, they could access multiple systems
3. To test the security of its system to find any weaknesses before others find them

Pages 54–55
1. Any four of the following: Windows 10, macOS, Unix, Chrome OS, BeOS, MS-Dos, Linux, Ubuntu
2. Multitasking
3. Examples of utilities: anti-virus, adware removers, disc defragmentation, file converters, compression utilities

Pages 56–59 Review Questions
Computer Networking

Wired and Wireless Networks 1
1. Any two of the following: to enable access to apps [1]; to enable the downloading of programme guides [1]; to obtain firmware updates [1]; to enable connection to streaming services [1]
2. Switch [1]
3. False [1]
4. The amount of data that can pass between two network devices, measured in bits per second (bps) [1]
5. Microwave [1]
6. Any two of the following: a user account can be managed remotely [1]; the processing workload is reduced [1]; backups can be created from a central source [1]
7. Classroom resources and teaching materials can be shared [1]
8. A user on the network can access the contents of any other user's computer on the same network [1]

Wired and Wireless Networks 2
1. Switch [1]; router [1]
2. True [1]
3. Wireless access point [1]
4. Bluetooth [1]
5. 1990s [1]
6. Router [1]
7. Data can be sent over much longer distances [1]
8. Without access to the Internet the business cannot access its files [1]; all computer devices within the business must have Internet connectivity [1]
9. Websites are given user-friendly text addresses rather than a multi-digit IP address [1]

Network Topologies
1. Mesh network [1]
2. Star network [1]
3. D [1]
4. Star – If the server fails then the whole network will collapse
   Mesh – Managing the network requires a high level of network expertise [2]
5. Router [1]

Protocols and Layers
1. Bluetooth [1]
2. Hardware standards [1]
3. WPA3 [1]
4. Hexadecimal [1]
5. IP address [1]
6. IMAP [1]
7. Application layer [1]
8. Wi-Fi certified [1]
9. Any two of the following: audio file [1]; image file [1]; web page [1]; video file [1]; operating system [1]
10. When a static IP address is assigned to a computer by an external provider it is fixed and cannot be changed [1]. A dynamic address is usually assigned within a network and can change as new devices are added or if the network is restarted [1]

Pages 60–63 Practice Questions
System Security and Software

Common System Threats
1. Any three of the following: usernames [1]; passwords [1]; dates of birth [1]; family details [1]; pet names [1]; locations [1]; bank account details [1]
2. Password [1]; social network [1]; bank [1]; hacker [1]; accounts [1]
3. Malicious software [2]
4. Trojan or Trojan horse software [1]
5. Worm [1]
6. To lock a user out of a system or their files [1] until a fee is paid to the creator of the malware [1]
7. Phishing [1]; shouldering [1]; blagging [1]
8. Watching a user at an ATM [1] and recording their PIN details [1]
9. It is carried out face to face [1]
10. It repeatedly [1] tries different usernames and passwords to attempt to access a system [1]
11. Denial [1] of service [1]
12. Data interception and theft [1]

Threat Prevention
1. To ensure that it is up to date with all of the latest threats [1]
2. Encryption [1]
3. Firewall [1]
4. Physical security – A practical way to protect equipment and data from external attackers
   Encryption – Converts information into a meaningless form that cannot be read if intercepted
   Penetration testing – Searching for potential weaknesses in a system that could be exploited [3]
5. They might have different roles with different levels of security access [1]

6. The users [1]
7. B [1]; D [1]

System Software
1. Hardware [1]; software [1]; user [1]
2. Buffer [1]
3. Any four of the following: scanner [1]; printer [1]; speaker [1]; webcam [1]; microphone [1]; graphics tablet [1]
4. A mouse [1]
5. It may stop working [1]
6. Supports [1]; system security [1]; management [1]
7. The reduction in size of a file so that it takes up less disk space [1]
8. Defragmentation [1]
9. Account creation [1]; access rights [1]; security privileges [1]

Pages 64–69 **Revise Questions**

Pages 64–65
1. Examples: use of social network posts; GPS tagging of photos; use of online shopping services; unencrypted emails; mobile phone signal locations; accessing open Wi-Fi networks
2. Examples: in high-angle camera fire and rescue services; for video recording of extreme sports; in film-making – much cheaper than filming from a helicopter; military use
3. Risks of being infected with malware from websites; breaking copyright law without knowledge; original content creators not being paid for their efforts

Pages 66–67
1. By reducing the amount of computer hardware e-waste disposed of in landfill sites; older machines with a lower specification can still be used in developing countries; by reducing the use of rare metals and minerals
2. Potential for accidents if a computer fails; questions about who would be responsible in the case of accidents; how standard and driverless cars will exist together on the same roads; and what the charging and power requirements of driverless cars will be
3. Any five of the following: copper; gold; platinum; silver; tungsten; neodymium; terbium; dysprosium

Pages 68–69
1. Computer Misuse Act 1990
2. As open source software is normally provided at no cost
3. Data Protection Act 2018

Pages 70–73 **Review Questions**
System Security and Software

Common System Threats
1. Home life [1]; education [1]; workplace [1]
2. Your personal files may be copied to the creator [1]; your keystrokes may be recorded, giving away usernames and passwords [1]

---

3. Pharming [1]
4. Virus [1]
5. It constantly displays targeted advertising [1] and redirects search requests without permission [1]
6. Phishing [1]
7. Any one of the following: they may not have been informed about computer scams [1]; they may not have much computer experience [1]
8. Any two of the following: at a petrol station [1]; at a shop till [1]; in a restaurant [1]; at an office computer [1]
9. Any three of the following: usernames [1]; passwords [1]; personal details [1]; PIN details [1]; bank or credit card numbers [1]
10. Any two from the following: a ransom for payment [1]; change to a websites content [1]; access to secure information [1]
11. Structured [1] Query [1] Language [1]
12. Commands written in SQL are used [1] instead of usernames and passwords [1] to access and steal private information [1]

Threat Prevention
1. Any three of the following: Trojan [1]; spyware [1]; adware [1]; worms [1]; viruses [1]
2. Hardware based [1]
3. To prevent message data being intercepted [1] and used for criminal purposes [1]
4. Any three of the following: penetration testing [1]; anti-malware [1]; firewalls [1]; user access levels [1]; passwords [1]; encryption [1]; physical security [1]
5. To ensure that customer details are kept secure [1] and to prevent customer details from being used for criminal purposes [1]
6. Files can be copied on to or removed from the network without permission [1] and files may contain malware [1]
7. Reading a file means that it can be viewed only and no changes can be made [1]. Write access allows the file to be edited or changed and resaved [1]
8. It can be forgotten, preventing access [1]
9. A [1]; F [1]
10. If the password is discovered by a hacker, they have less time to access personal data (such as bank details) [1]
11. Hackers can use software to automatically try all dictionary words to crack passwords [1]

System Software
1. Any three of the following: smartphone [1]; desktop computer [1]; laptop [1]; tablet [1]
2. Any three of the following: Windows 10 [1]; MacOS [1]; Unix [1]; Chrome OS [1]; BeOS [1]; MS-Dos [1]; Linux [1]; Ubuntu [1]
3. Command line prompt or interface [1]

---

4. Any two of the following: drag and drop [1]; menu systems [1]; mouse-controlled cursor [1]
5. The ability to have more than one user account on the same computer [1]
6. Users can have their own files and folders [1] and specified levels of access to programs and settings [1]
7. Software applications created by an external organisation or programmer but designed to run in conjunction with the OS [1]
8. So that if data is accessed, it cannot be understood (because it is in code) [1]
9. Any three of the following: image [1]; text [1]; audio [1]; video [1]
10. Defragmentation software [1] it re-organises the files on the disk for quicker access [1].
11. A [1]

Pages 74–77 **Practice Questions**
Ethical, Legal, Cultural and
Environmental Concerns

Ethical and Legal Concerns
1. Global Positioning System [1]
2. Cookies are accessible data files, saved on our computer [1], that contain our Internet history [1]
3. Examples: What are social networks doing with all the data they hold about us? [1]; Should mobile phones and/or Internet records be checked by government agencies? [1]; Should our Internet access be more restricted? [1]
4. Robots can operate 24/7 [1]; tasks are repeated precisely [1]
5. The ability to sell products across the world [1]; the ability to hide one's identity [1]
6. Copyright laws [1]
7. To prevent acts of terrorism [1]
8. Those creating abusive messages and material can be tracked back to their own computer [1]
9. Fun: filming active sports (or similar) [1]; commercial: potential delivery system [1]; government: surveillance or pilotless combat [1]
10. Personal information can be used to access other accounts [1] and guess our passwords [1]

Cultural and Environmental Concerns
1. Any three of the following: communication [1]; health [1]; transport [1]; education [1]; leisure activities [1]; employment [1]
2. Any two of the following: lack of access to technology [1]; financial constraints – being unable to buy the latest technology [1]; geographical constraints – restricted Internet access in rural areas [1]

3.

Impact	Positive	Negative
Replacement of physical media with downloads.	✓	
Cost of the transportation of raw and synthetic materials for the production of smart devices.		✓
The development of renewable energy sources.	✓	

[3]

4. It can be accessed anywhere in the world by anyone with an Internet connection [1]
5. Because of the wide range of materials used to create them, which often includes rare elements [1]
6. Benefits: fewer accidents, as traffic flow is controlled [1]; driver mistakes are reduced [1]; efficient navigation reduces travel time [1]. Drawbacks: lack of customer trust [1]; potential for high-speed crashes [1]; complexity and increased cost [1]
7. Making the player feel as if they are part of the game [1]
8. Any one of the following: lack of telephone line access [1]; lack of mains electricity [1]; lack of mobile phone coverage [1]
9. Any two of the following: saving trees [1], which helps to reduce greenhouse gases [1]; reduction of paper transportation costs [1]

Computer Science Legislation

1. Any three of the following:
   Data should be used fairly, lawfully and transparently [1]
   Data must be obtained and used only for specified purposes. [1]
   Data shall be adequate, relevant and not excessive. [1]
   Data should be accurate and kept up to date. [1]
   Data should not be kept for longer than necessary. [1]
   Data must be kept safe and secure. [1]
   Those organisations working with our data are accountable for all data protection and must produce evidence of their compliance. [1]
2. Computer Misuse Act 1990 [1]
3. That only required data is stored [1]
4. Copyright, Designs and Patents Act 1988 [1]
5. Hacking [1]
6. False [1]
7. Data Protection Act 2018 [1]
8. Any person whose details are held on an organisation's computer system [1]
9. Computer Misuse Act 1990 [1]
10. Any three of: price [1]; ease of use [1]; familiarity [1]; operating system [1]

Pages 78–79
1. The problem to be solved
2. Abstraction

Pages 80–81
1. Binary search
2. Bubble sort

Pages 82–83
1. The act of repeating any process until a specified result is achieved
2. Examples include days of the week, hours/minutes in a day, pi and degrees in a circle

Pages 84–85
1. A single equals sign is used for the definition of variables
2. $x = 2$
3. False

Pages 86–87
1. An OR gate
2. A NOT gate
3. 8

Ethical and Legal Concerns
1. Ethical use of computer technology means trying to cause no harm to others [1] and acting in a morally correct way to improve society [1]
2. So that they can use our location to customise the application or suggest local services [1]
3. The application may pass our contact details on to third parties [1]
4. Positive: jobs are created to build and program the robots [1]; negative: robots may replace manual labourers [1]
5. They must constantly train staff to try to keep up with the latest cybercrime methods [1]
6. Illegal music and video streaming sites are easy to access [1] without parental knowledge or knowledge of copyright laws [1]
7. Any two of the following: it is too easy to access illegal or copyrighted material [1]; we can become victims of hackers and malware without our knowledge [1]; there are scams and false information on the Internet [1]; there is a lack of age-related content controls [1]

Cultural and Environmental Concerns
1. Positive: jobs can be applied for quickly and around the world from home [1]; negative: those without reliable Internet access or the ability to use the Internet miss out [1]
2. Any three of the following: reductions in the use of paper [1]; reductions in material costs from the use of downloads instead of physical media [1]; mobile and home working reduces transportation costs [1]; smarter devices control their energy usage to meet our needs, reducing wastage [1]; the development of increasingly efficient renewable energy production [1]
3. Either of the following: they did not grow up with computer technology [1]; computer technology was not part of their education, unlike children today [1]
4. Lack of power and/or infrastructure [1]; lack of Internet connectivity [1]

5. Any computer-related technology that cannot be recycled easily [1]
6. One teacher can stream a single lesson to multiple classrooms at once [1]
7. Virtual reality headset [1]
8. Users do not keep their devices for their full lifetime [1]; the manufacturing of new devices increases energy consumption and the release of greenhouse gases [1]
9. Doctors can share results and ideas all around the world, allowing them to pool their knowledge [1]

Computer Science Legislation
1. Two singers disagree about ownership of a song – Copyright, Designs and Patents Act 1988
   An employee takes a company's customer database to a new company – Data Protection Act 2018
   An online email server is hacked and personal messages are stolen – Computer Misuse Act 1990 [3]
2. Data Protection Act 2018 [1]
3. Open source software can be shared and edited without limits [1], whereas proprietary software is owned by its creator and can be used only with permission or through a licence [1]
4. Films [1]; music [1]; games [1]; books [1]
5. Data must be easily accessible by the owners [1] and organisations must be clear about how they process data [1]
6. Computer Misuse Act 1990 [1]
7. Companies should have updated their records for the previous family [1] and deleted them if they were no longer required [1]
8. Identify any copyright terms in relation to the images [1] and contact the owner, if required, to gain permission to use the images [1]

Algorithms and Flowcharts
1. An algorithm is a step-by-step sequence of instructions [1] to solve a problem or carry out a task [1]
2. Decomposition – The process of breaking tasks into smaller tasks that are easier to understand and then solve.
   Abstraction – The removal of unwanted or unnecessary information from a task. This allows focus and clarity when solving problems.
   Algorithmic thinking – Being able to imagine a solution to a problem in a series of logical steps. [3]
3. Output [1]
4. Diamond [1]
5. [5]

Shape	Description
⬭	Used at the start or end point of a flow diagram.
▱	Used to represent the input or output of data in a process.
◇	Used when a decision or choice must be made.

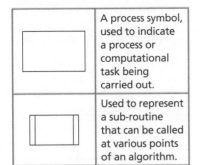

	A process symbol, used to indicate a process or computational task being carried out.
	Used to represent a sub-routine that can be called at various points of an algorithm.

Searching and Sorting Algorithms

1. Linear search [1], as it examines each value in turn until a match is found [1]
2. The first two values in a list are compared with each other [1] and the larger is placed first in the list [1]. The next pair of values is then checked, swapped if required, and so on, until the values are listed in descending order [1]
3. Merge sort [1]; insertion sort [1]

Pseudocode 1

1. Pseudocode uses simple English terminology and syntax [1]. It is not designed to be run by a computer and so simple errors are allowed [1]
2. if – Used in a question, as part of a decision process
   else – To provide a response if a statement is not met
   then – To provide a response if a statement is met
   while – A loop with a condition set at the start
   print – To display a response on screen to the user
   input – Requires an entry from the user in response to a question
   for – Used to create a counting loop [7]
3. So that variables and functions are easily identifiable [1]
4.

Value	Variable	Constant
numberCars = 19	✓	
daysofYear = 365		✓
hoursinDay = 24		✓
penWidth = 5	✓	

[4]
5. It allows personal notes to be added to coding to explain thinking [1]
6. Example:
```
colour = input("What is your favourite colour?")
print(colour,", that's my favourite colour too, good choice")
```
[2]

7. Example:
```
while answer! = "7"
    answer = input("How many days are in a week?")
endwhile
do
    answer = input("How many days are in a week?")
until answer == "7"
```
[4]

Pseudocode 2

1. a) Exactly equal to [1]
   b) Not equal to [1]
   c) Less than [1]
   d) Less than or equal to [1]
   e) Greater than [1]
   f) Greater than or equal to [1]
2. MOD (modulus) [1]
3. Exponentiation [1]; 27 [1]
4. AND [1]; OR [1]; NOT [1]
5. DIV [1]
6. a) 24 [1]
   b) 729 [1]
   c) 1 [1]
   d) 1 [1]
7. Example:
```
low = 15
high = 25
temp = input("What is the temperature outside?")
if temp > = low OR <= high
    print("Perfect!")
else
    print("Not quite right")
endif
```
[4]

Boolean Logic

1. Transistor [1]
2.

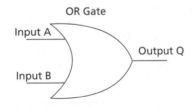

AND Gate

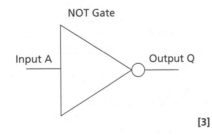

OR Gate

NOT Gate
[3]

3.

Inputs		Output
A	B	Q
0	0	0
1	0	1
0	1	1
1	1	1

[4]

4. a)

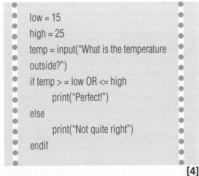

Inputs			Output
A	B	C	X
0	0	0	0
0	1	0	0
1	0	0	0
1	1	0	0
0	0	1	0
0	1	1	0
1	0	0	0
1	1	1	1

[8]

b)

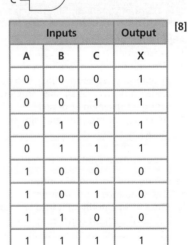

Inputs			Output
A	B	C	X
0	0	0	1
0	0	1	1
0	1	0	1
0	1	1	1
1	0	0	0
1	0	1	0
1	1	0	0
1	1	1	1

[8]

5. [8]

Inputs			Output
A	B	C	X
0	0	0	1
0	0	1	1
0	1	0	1
0	1	1	1
1	0	0	0
1	0	1	1
1	1	0	1
1	1	1	1

Pages 96–105 Revise Questions

Pages 96–97
1. Real (or float) data
2. Concatenation
3. Write mode

Pages 98–99
1. A primary key
2. 1
3. SELECT firstName FROM addressBook

Pages 100–101
1. Time and avoiding repetitive code
2. Functions

Pages 102–103
1. To allow for specific functionality for each user and to prevent clashes caused by multiple logins
2. Syntax error and logic error

Pages 104–105
1. Machine code
2. Interpreter
3. Examples include Java, JavaScript, Visual Basic, C++, Ruby, BASIC and Python

Pages 106–109 Review Questions
Algorithms and Computational Logic

Algorithms and Flowcharts
1. Abstraction [1]
2. Structure diagrams are used to graphically represent a problem and break it down into smaller problems using a top-down approach. [3]
3. To represent the flow and direction of data [1]
4. Sub-program [1]
5. Input/output symbol (parallelogram) [1]

Searching and Sorting Algorithms
1. The sequence is not ordered [1]
2. Data is repeatedly split into two halves [1] until each list contains only one item [1]. The items are then merged back together into the order required [1]

Pseudocode 1
1. for / while [1]
2. Naming conventions [1]
3. Constant [1]
4. 100 [1]
5. // This closes the program [1]
6. It states the correct answer is B [1]. The user is asked to type in an answer [1]. Until the correct answer B is typed in, it will keep repeating "Try again" [1].

Pseudocode 2
1. Comparison [1]
2. Boolean operators – Used to define relationships using logical operators
   Arithmetic operators – Used for mathematical calculations in pseudocode
   Comparison operators – Used to test the relationship between two values [3]
3. The single equals sign = is used to define a variable [1]. The double equals sign == means exactly equal to when testing relationships [1]
4. a) < [1]
   b) > [1]
   c) <= [1]
   d) >= [1]
5. MOD [1]
6. OR [1]
7. Trace table [1]

Boolean Logic
1. NOT gate [1]
2.

Inputs		Output
A	B	Q
0	0	0
1	0	0
0	1	0
1	1	1

[4]

3. B and C are inputs and X is an output [2]
4. Turned on [1]
5. 16 [1]
6. OR gate [1]
7. Off and on, respectively [2]

Pages 110–113 Practice Questions
Programming Techniques, Programs, Translators and Languages

Programming Techniques 1
1. Integer – A whole number with no decimal point
   Boolean – Digital data – can present only two values
   Real (or float) – All numbers, including those with a decimal point
   Character – A single letter, number or symbol
   String – A collection of alphanumeric data characters and symbols [5]
2. Real data [1]
3. The conversion of one data type into another [1]
4. To convert the number 42 into a string [1]
5. Quotation marks [1]
6. Concatenation [1]
7. openRead will simply open an existing file in read-only mode [1], whereas openWrite will create a new file or overwrite an existing file [1]
8. `endOfFile()` [1]
9. It would open the file called petNames.txt [1], replace the contents with the name Poppy [1] and close the file [1]

Programming Techniques 2
1. Data [1]; tables [1]; fields [1]; records [1]; primary key [1]

2. A flat-file database has only one table [1], whereas a relational database has multiple tables, linked together by a common key field [1]
3. Structured Query Language [1]
4. Search for a student with an examination score of greater than 80 [1] and display their surname [1] from a table called Classlist [1]
5. diceThrow [1] = random(1,6) [1]

Programming Techniques 3
1. An array is a data structure for storing groups within a program [1], meaning that several pieces of data can be stored under one name or variable [1]
2. Two-dimensional array [1]
3. Parameters [1]
4. Procedures [1] and functions [1]

Producing Robust Programs
1. Use of authentication to check the identity of a user [1]; use of passwords to prevent unauthorised access [1]; user access linked to usernames/passwords [1]; plan for users making mistakes [1]
2. Input validation [1]
3. Use of indentation [1], naming conventions [1] and sub-programs [1]
4. Iterative testing [1]
5. Syntax error [1]
6. Normal data – Acceptable data likely to be input into the program
   Boundary data – Values at the limit of what a program can handle
   Erroneous data – Values the program should not accept or process [3]
7. A test plan should spot program errors and potential user problems [1] before the program is released commercially to help prevent poor customer reviews [1]
8. Any five of the following: test number [1]; test description/reason [1]; test data to be used [1]; expected outcome [1]; actual outcome [1]; further action if required [1]

Languages, Translators and Integrated Development Environments
1. Humans use high-level languages to write programs, which must then be translated before a computer can understand them [1], whereas low-level languages are much closer to a format that a computer can understand [1]
2. Binary [1]
3. Machine code [1]
4. It translates any programming language [1] other than machine code into a format that a computer can understand [1]
5. Machine code – an example of a low-level language that can execute commands directly without any translation
   Compilers – Used to read high-level languages and convert programs as a whole into machine code programs
   Interpreters – Examine high-level language files one line at a time and convert each instruction into compatible machine code instructions [3]
6. Integrated development environment [1]

7. Code editor [1]; carrying out error diagnostics [1]; providing a run-time environment [1]; translator [1]
8. Code editor or text editor [1]

Programming Techniques 1
1. a) int [1]
   b) bool [1]
   c) real (or float) [1]
   d) char [1]
   e) str [1]
2. Character [1]
3. Casting or typecasting [1]
4.
```
string1 = "Good morning
Dave"
print(string1)
```
[1]
[1]
5. Concatenation [1]
6. a) 12 (number of characters) [1]
   b) HELLO WORLD! [1]
   c) The fourth character 'l' [1]
7. It will overwrite the contents of the file [1]

Programming Techniques 2
1. identNumber [1] because the primary key needs to be unique [1]
2. A common key field [1]
3. This is a language [1] designed to create, edit and search databases [1]
4. It is used to limit, or set a condition, on the amount of data returned [1]

Programming Techniques 3
1. Example:
```
array season[4]
season[0] = "Winter"
season[1] = "Spring"
season[2] = "Summer"
season[3] = "Autumn"
```
[2]
2. Example:
```
temp = ["21","24","26","28"]
```
[3]
3. Example:
```
Survey [3,3]
Survey = [[7, "6","9"],
[7, "4","3"],
[7, "6","6"]]
```
[4]
4. Row 0, column 2: 9 [1]
5. A procedure is a named group of instructions that is used as required to complete a set task, whereas a function is a group of instructions designed to return a value. [2]

Producing Robust Programs
1. Defensive design [1]
2. Program maintainability [1]
3. D [1]
4. C [1]; it should be clear to the reader what the content of the variable will be [1]
5. Final / Terminal testing [1]
6. Syntax error [1]
7. a) 10 [1]
   b) 1 or 12 [1]
   c) 15 [1]

8. Expected outcome is what you imagine should happen if the program is run, based on your planning [1]. Actual outcome is what happens when the program is run for the first time [1].

Languages, Translators and Integrated Development Environments
1. Because low-level languages are much closer to direct instructions that a computer can understand, whereas high-level languages are written by humans and contain keywords and syntax that programmers understand [1]
2. Used to read high-level languages and convert programs as a whole into machine code programs [1]
3. Because a compiler converts a whole program at once [1]
4. Compiler [1]
5. Programs can be written and tested [1] without potentially causing damage to complex machinery [1]
6. Run-time environment [1]

1. Any two of the following: error diagnostics [1]; run-time environment [1]; editor [1]; translator [1]
2. 01110001 [2], 113 [1]
3. Input signals through pressing the screen [1] and visual output via the screen [1]
4. Ransomware locks or disables a computer [1] and payment is demanded to return the computer to normal [1]
5. The Internet is a global network of connected networks [1] and the World Wide Web is a collection of websites hosted on these networks [1]
6.
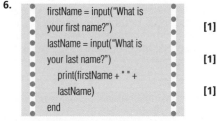
```
firstName = input("What is
your first name?")
lastName = input("What is
your last name?")
    print(firstName + " " +
lastName)
end
```
[1]
[1]
[1]
7. To prevent the duplication of numbers [1]
8. A compiler translates the program all in one go [1] and an interpreter translates one line at a time [1]
9. Any three of the following: anti-malware [1]; firewalls [1]; user access levels [1]; passwords [1]; encryption [1]; physical security [1]
10. Example answer:
```
procedure imageCheck
maxfileSize = 1
    fileSize = input("Please
    upload file")
if filesize <= maxfileSize
    then upload
else
    print("File too large")
end
```
[1]
[1]
[1]
[1]
[1]
[1]

11. The operating system needs to run on different devices [1], created by different manufacturers [1]
12. comments [1]; indentation [1]; naming conventions [1]; sub-programs [1]
13. bit, nibble, byte, MB, GB, PB [1]
14. WEP, WPA, WPA2, WPA3 [1]; they should use WPA3 [1] as it is the newest [1]
15. Any four of the following: capacity/size [1]; speed [1]; portability [1]; durability [1]; reliability [1]; cost [1]
16. A record is one complete entry in a database [1], whereas a field is one element of a record [1].
17. Virtual memory is created by the operating system on the system hard drive [1] when RAM is full [1].
18. Answers similar to the following: Anticipating misuse [1] – users may misuse the site or try and download without paying [1]; authentication [1] – user accounts and passwords should be used [1]
19. Any four of the following: new devices can be added [1]; central management [1]; less chance of data clashes [1]; failing devices will not break the system [1]; data can be targeted at particular devices [1]
20. 57, 32, 4, 5, 40, 54, 2 = start
    57, 32, 4, 5   40, 54, 2
    57, 32,   4, 5   40, 54,   2
    57 32 4 5 40 54 2 [1]
    32, 57 4, 5 40, 54 2
    4, 5, 32, 57   2, 40, 54 [1]
    2, 4, 5, 32, 40, 54, 57 = finish
21. An embedded system is a computer system with a specific purpose [1] that is built into a larger system [1]
22. A single equals sign is used to define variables [1] and a double equals sign is used in comparisons to represent exactly equal to [1]
23. Any two of the following: cloud-based systems offer additional storage [1], giving more space for student document folders [1]
    Backup systems are often included in cloud-based systems [1], saving time [1]
    Cloud-based systems offer opportunities for home working [1] for students and staff [1]
    Less network expertise needed to use cloud-based systems [1], saving the school money [1]
24. To ensure that there are enough characters available [1] to encode all of the spoken languages in the world [1]
25. The program will have an organised structure [1] and each note can be called upon when required, limiting the repetition of code [1]
26. False [1]
27. HTTPS means that the website has secure encryption [1], protecting his private information when shopping [1]
28. a) memberID [1]
    b) To make sure that each record has a uniquely identifiable field that can be searched for [1]
29. Volatile memory, for example RAM [1], will hold data in memory only if there is a power source [1], whereas non-volatile memory, for example USB storage [1], will keep the contents in memory when power is disconnected [1]

30. 14, 22, 12, 18 - start
14, 12, 18, 22 - first pass
12, 14, 18, 22 - second pass
12, 14, 18, 22 - final pass (no swaps) **[2]**
31. Abstraction is the removal of unwanted or unnecessary information from a task **[1]**, providing focus and clarity **[1]**
32. Any three of the following: dishwasher **[1]**; MP3 player **[1]**; washing machine **[1]**; mobile phone **[1]**; home entertainment systems **[1]**; or similar
33. Unknowingly sharing her files **[1]**; dangers from malware in downloaded files **[1]**; downloading copyrighted material **[1]**
34. Example answers:
Normal: 04/05/1977 **[1]**
Boundary: 01/01/1900 or 31/12/2018 **[1]**
Erroneous: 5th June 1969 **[1]**
35. False **[1]**
36. Devices are built using rare resources **[1]** that require additional energy to manufacture **[1]**, creating additional e-waste **[1]** and toxic waste that can leak into the environment **[1]**.
37. Phishing uses email, text messages and phone calls to impersonate, for example, a financial organisation and ask users to confirm or divulge their personal details **[1]**. Shouldering is the technique of watching a user at an ATM and recording their PIN details **[1]**. Blagging is carried out face to face and uses believable scenarios to trick people into giving up their personal information **[1]**
38. Any three of the following: files on the hard drive are moved **[1]**; empty spaces are collected together **[1]**; files are moved to be stored together **[1]**; fewer disk accesses are needed **[1]**
39. A denial of service attack tries to flood a website or network with data traffic to bring it to a halt **[1]**. Such attacks are often used to demand a ransom or a change in policy **[1]**
40. True **[1]**
41. a) Least significant bit **[1]**; Most significant bit **[1]**
b) <u>MSB</u> 10110101 <u>LSB</u> **[1]**
42. A Domain Name Service is made up of multiple Domain Name Servers. **[1]**
43. A local variable is specified within a sub-program and can only be used within it **[1]**. A global variable can be referred to within the whole program, including sub-programs **[1]**
44. Any two, or similar, from the following: days of the week **[1]**; days in the year **[1]**; number of months **[1]**; hours in the day **[1]**

Glossary

8-bit – A binary number of eight characters representing the values 0–255.

Abstraction – The removal of unwanted or unnecessary information from a task or problem to provide focus.

Accumulator – Temporarily stores the results of calculations carried out by the ALU.

Adware – A form of spyware designed to automatically open or generate advertisements.

Algorithm – A sequence of step-by-step instructions to solve a problem or carry out a task.

Algorithmic thinking – Being able to imagine a solution to a problem in a series of logical steps.

Alphanumeric – A data type where any combination of letters and numbers from the keyboard is acceptable.

Analogue – A continuous signal that cannot be directly processed by a computer.

Anti-malware – Software designed to stop and remove malicious software from a system.

Anticipating misuse – Predicting the types of misuse that might happen to a system in order to prevent it.

Arguments – The data used by a sub-program.

Arithmetic logic unit (ALU) – The part of the CPU that carries out calculations.

ASCII – A common coding standard of 128 characters for computer manufacturers to share.

Authentication – Checking the identify of a user, normally with a username and password.

Bandwidth – The amount of data that can pass between two network devices per second.

Base 2 – A two-digit number system comprising 1 and 0; used to represent binary.

Base 10 – Our standard decimal numbering system.

Base 16 – A number system with 16 characters of numbers and letters, also known as hexadecimal.

BASIC – A simple high-level programming language, often used by beginners.

Binary – A base 2 number system using two digits: 1 and 0.

Binary search – Looks for a specific value in an ordered list by comparing it to the others around it.

Binary shift – The movement of bits in a binary sequence left and right to represent multiplication and division.

BIOS – Basic input/output system; computer start-up software stored in ROM.

Bit depth – The number of bits used to encode each sample; the higher the bit depth, the higher the quality of the audio.

Blagging – The act of using believable scenarios to trick people into giving up personal information.

Blogs – Websites based around the creation of chronological entries or posts.

Bluetooth – A wireless short-range personal network.

Boolean – Data that can have one of only two values, for example: 1/0, true/false.

Boolean operators – Use of AND, OR and NOT to connect and define relationships between data values or search terms.

Boundary data – Values at the limit of what a program should be able to handle.

Brute force attack – Repeatedly trying different usernames and passwords in an attempt to access a system.

Bubble sort – Repeatedly compares adjacent pairs of values in a list and swaps until all items are in order.

Buffers – An allocation of free memory for a temporary task.

Bus – The connection and transfer of data between devices in a computer system.

Cache – Quick-to-access memory stored within the CPU.

Casting – In programming, the conversion of one data type into another.

Central processing unit (CPU) – The core of a computer system that processes and controls the flow of data.

C Family – A group of high-level programming languages.

Character – A single letter, number or symbol in a program.

Character sets – Alphanumeric characters and symbols, converted into a computer-readable binary equivalent.

Client – A computer or workstation that receives information from a central server.

Client–server – A network where a main computer server is accessed from multiple client computers.

Clock speed – The rate in gigahertz per second at which instructions are processed by the CPU.

Cloud computing – The remote storing and accessibility of files and applications via the Internet.

Colour depth – The number of bits per pixel in an electronic image.

Comparison operators – Operators, such as < and ==, used by programmers to test the relationship between two values.

Compilers – Used to read high-level languages and convert programs as a whole into machine code.

Compression – See Data compression.

Computational thinking – Breaking a problem down in a logical, structured way.

Concatenation – The joining together of two strings in a program.

Constant – A value that cannot be changed or edited within a running program.

Control unit – The part of the CPU that controls the flow of data both in and around the CPU.

Cookies – Small files stored on computers, accessible by web servers, that contain Internet browsing data.

Copyrighted – The ownership rights of the original creator of any original content.

Cores – The processing units found inside a CPU; each core can carry out a separate task.

Cypher – A method of encrypting or decrypting text.

Dark web – Areas of the World Wide Web that are hidden from normal searches, and only accessible via specialist browser software.

Databases – Systems for storing large amounts of data, categorised and structured for ease of accessibility.

Data compression – The process of reducing the file size of an electronic file.

Data interception and theft – Intercepting and decoding a message containing sensitive information before it reaches its destination.

Decomposition – The process of breaking tasks into smaller tasks that are easier to understand and then solve.

Defragmentation – Re-organising the data on a hard drive to speed up access and free up storage space.

Delphi – A high-level programming language, used to develop desktop, mobile and web applications.

Denary – Also known as decimal, a base 10 number system.

Denial of service attack – Flooding a website or network with data traffic to bring it to a halt.

Digital divide – The social and economic gap between those who have and those who do not have access to computer technology.

Domain Name Server – Web servers around the world that are part of the Domain Name Service.

Domain Name Service – An Internet naming service that links a numerical network IP addresses with a familiar text-based website address.

Drivers – Small programs that control a particular device within a computer system.

Embedded system – A small computer system with a specific purpose that is built into a larger device.

Encryption – The conversion of important data into a form that cannot be read without a key.

Erroneous data – Data that should be rejected by a system as it is of the incorrect data type.

Error diagnostics – Also referred to as debugging tools, used to identify errors in particular lines of code.

Ethernet – A cable used to connect NICs, routers and switches.

Exponentiation – A pseudocode arithmetic operator that assigns one value to the power of another.

Fields – A category within a database.

File management – The organisation of files and documents to allow for easy access and retrieval.

File server – Provides shared access to files hosted on a specific network computer.

Final/terminal testing – Testing carried out when a program is complete, and it can be tested by real users.

Firewalls – Hardware or software designed to protect a system from unauthorised access.

Flat-file database – A database with a single table and no links to other tables.

Flowchart – Visualises an algorithm and shows clearly the flow of information.

Functions – A type of sub-program designed to return a value that the program will use.

Global variable/constant – A value that can be referred to at any point in a program, including sub-programs.

GPS – Global Positioning System; a satellite-based navigation system that provides devices with an exact geographical location.

GPS location – A user's current position on the earth calculated using latitude and longitude coordinates.

Graphical user interface – A visual system, often cursor driven, that allows users to access and control a computer system.

Hardware standards – The use of common interface or charging sockets, motherboard compatibility and communication connectivity.

Hexadecimal – A base 16 number system of sixteen characters: 0–9 and A–F.

High-level languages – Programming languages, such as Python, containing keywords and syntax that programmers understand.

Homeworking – The transfer of workplace activities to the home.

Hosting – The storing of a website, or a similar file system, on a network computer accessible via the Internet.

Identifier – The name given to a variable so it can be identified in a program.

Immersive – A system designed to engage the user completely in an experience, often using three-dimensional headset technology.

Input – Any data entered into a system to be processed.

Input devices – Devices that provide an input signal into a computer system.

Input validation – Checks to make sure user data entered into a program is both accurate and in the correct data format.

Insertion sort – Repeatedly comparing each item in a list with the previous item and inserting it into the correct position.

Integer – A whole number in a program with no decimal point.

Internet Protocol – A unique identification address assigned to network devices to facilitate Internet connectivity.

Interpreters – Software that converts high-level language files one line at a time into compatible machine code.

Invalid data – Data that cannot be processed.

Iteration – Repeating a task a set number of times or until a certain condition is met.

Iterative testing – The program cycle of design, development and testing.

Java – A high-level programming language.

LAN – Local area network; computers are connected with the ability to share information in a small geographical area.

Layers – A set of network protocols grouped together with a specific purpose.

Least significant bit (LSB) – Has the lowest value and is the first number on the right of an 8-bit binary sequence.

Linear search – Compares each value in a list, one at a time, to a required value until a match is made.

Local variable/constant – A value that can only referred to within the sub-program it is declared.

Logic diagrams – Graphical representations of simple Boolean operations using gates.

Logic error – A fault in the structure or design of a program.

Lossless compression – The use of an algorithm to compress data but then reconstruct it without data loss.

Lossy compression – File size reduction by permanently removing data such as duplicated data elements.

Low-level languages – Programming languages that are closer to direct instructions that a computer can understand.

Machine code – A low-level programming language that can execute commands directly without any translation.

Malware – Short for malicious software: designed to cause damage or to steal information from the user.

Media access control – A hardwired address assigned to all network devices during manufacture.

Memory Address Register – The location address in memory of the next piece of data or instruction that the CPU needs.

Memory Data Register – A CPU register that stores instructions or pieces of data.

Memory management – The process of allocating free space and prioritising how much memory and resources the CPU and memory modules can use.

Merge sort – Data is repeatedly split into halves until single items remain, and is then reassembled in order.

Mesh network – A network topology in which every device within the network is connected to every other device.

Metadata – Additional file property data stored within a file, such as the date a photo was taken.

Modulus – A pseudocode arithmetic operator that returns the remainder after a division.

Most significant bit (MSB) – Has the largest value and is the first number on the left of an 8-bit binary sequence.

Multimedia – The combination of multiple media elements: text, sound, video, graphics and user interactivity.

Multitasking – A computer's ability to complete multiple processes at the same time.

Network storage – A secondary storage device that is accessed via network connectivity.

Nibble – 4 bits, half an 8-bit binary sequence.

Non-volatile – Memory that retains its contents even after power is switched off.

Normal data – Acceptable data a program is likely to accept and process.

One-dimensional array – A single list in a program of common elements.

Open source – Software created to be shared openly online at no cost or with no limits on how it can be used.

Operating system – Software designed to manage a computer system, control hardware and allow applications to be run.

Output – Data processed by a computer system and returned to the user.

Output devices – Devices that receive instructions or commands from a computer system and carry them out.

Overflow error – Occurs when a computer tries to process more bits than it is designed to handle.

Overwrite – To replace the contents of a file with new data.

Parameters – The variables used within a sub-program.

Passwords – Strings of characters, numbers, letters and symbols that allow access to a computer system.

Peer-to-peer – A network where all computers act as both client and server.

Penetration testing – The search for vulnerabilities within a system that could be exploited for criminal purposes.

Peripherals – Any piece of hardware connected to a computer, outside of the CPU and working memory.

Permissions – Individually set user access rights on a network.

Pharming – Redirecting a user's website request to a fraudulent site, by modifying their DNS entries.

Phishing – Impersonating an organisation and asking users to confirm or divulge personal details.

PHP – An open-source general purpose scripting language, often used in website development.

Physical security – Protects important network equipment or data by physically preventing access.

Primary key – A unique identifiable field within a database that cannot be repeated.

Primary storage – Describes the main memory component of a computer system, also referred to as main memory.

Private key – Required to open an encrypted message.

Procedure – A type of sub-program: a set of instructions grouped together and assigned a name.

Processes – Any calculations, validations or operations carried out on data inputted into system.

Program counter – Continuously provides the CPU with the memory address of the next instruction to be carried out.

Proprietary – Owned by the individual or company who created it; permission is usually through a purchased licence.

Protocols – Sets of rules devised for network-compatible devices to allow for effective communication.

Pseudocode – A shared programming language using simple English terms to plan programs.

Public encryption key – Used to encrypt a message to prevent interception; can only be opened with the private key.

Python – A high-level programming language.

Quotient – A pseudocode arithmetic operator that divides but returns only a whole number or integer.

RAM – Random access memory is temporary memory used to store data and instructions currently in use.

Random number generation – Using either pseudocode or a coding language, a computer selects a random number within a set range.

Ransomware – Software designed to lock a user out of their system until a ransom is paid to unlock it.

Real (or float) – A program data type; all numbers, including those with a decimal point.

Records – A single row or entry of related data in a database.

Refining algorithms – A process designed to improve efficiency and remove errors at all stages of program development.

Register – A quickly accessible CPU memory location that stores either memory locations or the actual data to be processed.

Relational database – Multiple databases, linked together by a common key field.

Resolution – The number of pixels used to represent an electronic image.

ROM – Read-only memory that provides a computer system with important instructions that do not change.

Routers – Devices that connect networks together and allow communication between them.

Run-time environment – Allows a program to be run and tested within an integrated development environment (IDE).

Sample rate – The number of samples taken each second.

Sampling – The process of converting analogue into digital.

Secondary storage – Refers to the external devices used to store programs, documents and files.

Selection – A decision that needs to be made before the next step can be carried out.

Sequence – Carrying out tasks in a step-by-step sequence.

Server – A dedicated device or software system to provide services or functionality to devices connected to it.

Shouldering – The technique of watching a user at an ATM and recording their PIN details.

Social engineering – Describes a range of methods used by con artists or criminals to access personal information.

Software standards – The use of common file types, operating systems and web browsing formats.

Source code – A set of instructions written by a programmer using a standard programming language.

Spyware – Malware specifically designed to secretly pass on user information to a third party.

SQL injection – The use of a common database programming language to access and steal information.

Standards – Allow different hardware manufacturers and software authors to create compatible cross-platform systems.

Star network – A network topology with a server at the centre and computers with network devices connected around it.

Storage capacity – The amount of data a device can store.

Streaming services – Internet-accessed multimedia content, presented to the user in real time as a constant data stream.

String – A collection of alphanumeric data characters and symbols, usually enclosed in quotation marks.

Structure diagrams – Used to graphically represent a problem and break it down into smaller problems using a top-level approach.

Structured Query Language – A programming language designed to create, edit and search databases.

Sub-program – A program section that can be called on at any time during a larger program to save time/avoid repetition.

Substring – A string created from an existing longer string. "Hello" is a substring of the string "Hello there".

Switches – Devices that provide network connectivity between other devices.

Syntax error – An error within a program that breaks the rules or grammar of the language in which it is written.

Test plan – A written plan of program tests, the results and how any errors might be resolved.

Third-party applications – Applications made by an external organisation not connected with the operating system or hardware.

Topology – The logical arrangement or physical structure of computers and network devices.

Trace table – Used to test an algorithm by examining each line of code step by step and predicting the results.

Transistors – Semiconducting devices used to amplify or switch electronic flow in a circuit.

Translators – Software designed to convert a programming language into machine code.

Trojan – Malware disguised as legitimate software, designed to cause damage or provide access to criminals.

Truth table – The representation of potential inputs and outputs (1s and 0s) in a logic diagram.

Two-dimensional array – An array that can be represented as a table with rows and columns where each element has a pair of numbers to locate it.

Unicode – A character set designed to contain all possible characters from all known languages.

User access levels – Individual permissions to limit the information users can access, read or edit.

User management – The management of users on a single computer within the same operating system.

Utility software – Used to carry out specific tasks to support an operating system.

Variable – A named location in memory used to store data that can change while a program is running.

Virtual memory – Created by the operating system on the hard drive if RAM becomes full.

Virus – Malware hidden within another program or file, designed to cause damage to file systems.

Visual Basic – A high-level programming language.

Volatile – Memory that loses all data stored when power is switched off (for example, RAM).

von Neumann architecture – A 'stored program' computer system containing both the computer program and the data it processes.

WAN – Wide area network; created by connecting one LAN to another across a geographical space.

Web server – Stores and hosts websites, and controls client access to the web pages stored on it.

Wired – A physical connection between devices.

Wired Equivalent Piracy (WEP) – The oldest and least secure Wi-Fi encryption standard.

Wireless – A connection between devices using radio waves.

Wi-Fi certified – An international standard for devices meeting industry-agreed network standards.

Wi-Fi Protected Access (WPA, WPA2 and WPA3) – A modern Wi-Fi encryption method.

Worm – Malware with the ability to independently replicate itself to spread between multiple connected systems.

Write – A file-handling mode enabling a new file to be created or an existing file to be overwritten.

Index

Collins

OCR GCSE 9-1

Computer Science

Workbook

Paul Clowrey

Preparing for the GCSE Exam

Revision That Really Works

Experts have found that there are two techniques that help you to retain and recall information and consistently produce better results in exams compared to other revision techniques.

It really isn't rocket science either – you simply need to:

- **test yourself** on each topic as many times as possible
- **leave a gap** between the test sessions.

Three Essential Revision Tips

1. Use Your Time Wisely

- Allow yourself plenty of time.
- Try to start revising six months before your exams – it's more effective and less stressful.
- Don't waste time re-reading the same information over and over again – it's not effective!

2. Make a Plan

- Identify all the topics you need to revise (this Complete Revision & Practice book will help you).
- Plan at least five sessions for each topic.
- One hour should be ample time to test yourself on the key ideas for a topic.
- Spread out the practice sessions for each topic – the optimum time to leave between each session is about one month but, if this isn't possible, just make the gaps as big as realistically possible.

3. Test Yourself

- Methods for testing yourself include: quizzes, practice questions, flashcards, past papers, explaining a topic to someone else.
- This Complete Revision & Practice book provides seven practice opportunities per topic.
- Don't worry if you get an answer wrong – provided you check what the correct answer is, you are more likely to get the same or similar questions right in future!

Visit **collins.co.uk/collinsGCSErevision** to download your free flashcards, for more information about the benefits of these revision techniques, and for further guidance on how to plan ahead and make them work for you.

Command Words used in Exam Questions

This table defines some of the most commonly used command words in GCSE exam questions.

Analyse	Focus on, and when possible break down, the key elements that can be used to build conclusions.
Complete	Provide any missing information or visual elements.
Convert	Change data from its original form to another.
Define	Precisely provide the meaning of a term, phrase or attribute.
Describe	Provide in your own words an account of a specific term, item or process.
Design	Create your own response to meet a defined set of requirements.
Explain	Describe with additional detail that supports and gives reasons for your answer.
How	In what way, or by what means, did something happen?
Identify	Make an informed choice from a range of possible answers.
Label	Add key terms or short descriptions to the diagram or graphic provided.
List	Provide one or more specific answers without elaboration.
State	Provide, without elaboration, a specific answer or example.

Contents

* Grading information is for guidance only and is not endorsed by the examination board.

Systems Architecture, Memory and Storage

The Purpose and Function of the Central Processing Unit

Grade 1–3

1 Match each term with its definition. **[3]**

| Input | | Programmed instructions for a computer with a specific task. |

| Output | | A device that sends information or data to the CPU. |

| Software | | Any physical device that would normally form part of a computer system. |

| Hardware | | A device that receives instructions or data from the CPU. |

Grade 4–6

2 Complete the representation of von Neumann architecture using the letters from the box. **[3]**

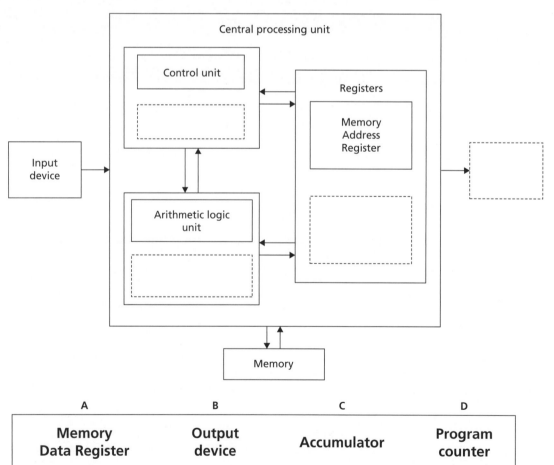

	A	B	C	D
	Memory Data Register	**Output device**	**Accumulator**	**Program counter**

Systems Architecture, Memory and Storage

3 Insert the missing word to complete the following sentence.

Registers either store .... locations or the actual data to be processed. **[1]**

4 In von Neumann architecture, what is meant by the term 'stored program'? **[2]**

5 Describe the relationship between the ALU and the accumulator. **[2]**

6 In von Neumann architecture, what part of the CPU is the program counter found in? **[1]**

Systems Architecture

1 Define the term 'clock speed'. **[1]**

2 A modern washing machine has embedded systems.

Describe **two** benefits that this might offer the manufacturer. **[2]**

3 The clock speed of modern CPUs has slowed in recent years. Instead, CPUs now have multiple cores.

Explain how this change has affected CPU performance. **[2]**

Systems Architecture, Memory and Storage

Grade 4–6

4 Briefly describe **four** stages of the fetch–decode–execute cycle. [4]

Grade 7–9

5 What is the difference between the L1 cache and the L2 cache? [2]

Grade 7–9

6 A computer gamer is finding that she has issues with her new console. Some games are crashing and it shuts down for no reason. She has been told it might be caused by one of the embedded systems.

Describe **two** disadvantages of multiple embedded systems in a device. [2]

Memory

Grade 1–3

1 In a modern computer system, what is the purpose of RAM? [1]

Grade 1–3

2 RAM is described as volatile, whereas ROM is described as non-volatile.

a) What do the terms 'volatile' and 'non-volatile' mean? [2]

b) Why is this difference important to computer manufacturers when they are designing BIOS? [1]

Systems Architecture, Memory and Storage

3 Define the term 'primary storage'. [1]

4 Primary storage is normally found on the motherboard.

State whether this statement is true or false. [1]

5 When a computer is booted, the BIOS runs.

a) What does the abbreviation BIOS stand for? [1]

b) State two tasks the BIOS carries out as the computer starts. [2]

6 Virtual memory is created by the operating system when required.

a) Why is virtual memory created? [1]

b) Where is virtual memory created? [1]

c) What problem can virtual memory cause? [1]

Systems Architecture, Memory and Storage

Storage Types, Devices and Characteristics

Grade 1–3

1 Describe **two** characteristics of magnetic storage that prevent it from being used in mobile devices such as smartphones and action cameras. **[2]**

Grade 4–6

2 A teacher is concerned about losing work. She is looking for a secondary storage device that will back up important files.

List **five** characteristics the teacher should consider when choosing a secondary storage device. **[5]**

Grade 4–6

3 Optical discs are a popular and cheap form of storage.

a) Name **three** different variations of optical disc. **[3]**

b) State **three** issues that should be considered when using optical discs. **[3]**

4 After many years of using his magnetic storage-based 120 GB MP3 player, Frank decides to upgrade to a 64 GB SSD-based model.

Describe **one** advantage that each device has over the other. **[2]**

....

....

....

5 Why would an optical drive not be suitable as the main storage for a laptop? **[2]**

....

....

....

6 Technology experts often warn users to think about the lifespan of storage media when considering file backup storage solutions.

Describe **one** way a user can prevent their current backup storage solution becoming outdated. **[1]**

....

....

Systems Architecture, Memory and Storage

Units and Formats of Data

Grade 4–6

1 Match each typical file type with its associated unit of data. [3]

high-definition video	terabytes
MP3 audio file	kilobytes
system backup files	megabytes
word processing document	gigabytes

Grade 4–6

2 What are the 8-bit ASCII numbers of the following characters?

a) The UK pound symbol [1]

b) The division symbol [1]

c) An upper-case K [1]

d) An exclamation mark [1]

Grade 7–9

3 What are 'control characters', 'printable characters' and 'symbols and punctuations' examples of? [1]

Grade 7–9

4 What is the name of the character set designed as a world industry standard? [1]

Grade 7–9

5 Why was an extra zero added to the original version of 7-bit ASCII? [2]

Systems Architecture, Memory and Storage

Video Solution   Question 1

Grade 7–9

6 State **three** non-printed commands that can be represented using a character set such as ASCII. **[3]**

....

....

....

Converting Data 1

Grade 1–3

1 Convert the following denary numbers into binary.

a) 18 **[1]**

....

b) 25 **[1]**

....

c) 251 **[1]**

....

d) 161 **[1]**

....

Grade 4–6

2 Add the following binary numbers and then convert the answer into denary.

a) 00000101 + 11100101 **[2]**

....

....

b) 00110101 + 00100100 **[2]**

....

....

Systems Architecture, Memory and Storage

Grade 4–6

3 Write a binary addition calculation that will result in a binary overflow. **[1]**

Grade 7–9

4 Carry out a left shift of 1 on the following binary numbers.

a) 00110101 **[1]**

b) 00100110 **[1]**

Grade 7–9

5 Carry out a right shift of 1 on the following binary numbers.

a) 11010100 **[1]**

b) 01011010 **[1]**

Grade 7–9

6 What is the practical purpose of using left and right shifts with binary numbers? **[1]**

Converting Data 2

Grade 4–6

1 Convert the following denary numbers into hexadecimal.

a) 254 **[1]**

b) 99 **[1]**

c) 42 **[1]**

Systems Architecture, Memory and Storage

Grade 4–6

2 Using the ASCII table, the word BIG can be represented in binary as:

01000010   **01001001**   **01000111**

Convert this binary sequence into a hexadecimal number sequence.   **[3]**

Grade 4–6

3 Convert the following hexadecimal numbers into denary.

a) 4F   **[1]**

b) 8C   **[1]**

c) 12   **[1]**

Grade 7–9

4 Why might a programmer claim that hexadecimal is easier to work with than binary?   **[1]**

Grade 7–9

5 What mistake might a new programmer make when working with the hexadecimal number 24?   **[1]**

Grade 7–9

6 If a computer can understand the binary number system, explain why it cannot understand hexadecimal.   **[2]**

Systems Architecture, Memory and Storage

Audio/Visual Formats and Compression

Grade 4–6

1 How many bits would be needed to create an image with:

a) 2 colours? [1]

b) 4 colours? [1]

c) 16 colours? [1]

Grade 4–6

2 State **two** ways in which a photo management program will use metadata. [2]

Grade 4–6

3 Why is the RAW image format popular with professional photographers? [1]

Grade 4–6

4 Audio podcasts are very popular with users of smartphones.

What file type is normally used, and why? [3]

Grade 7–9

5 Describe a benefit and a drawback of sampling an analogue audio recording at a very high bit depth. [2]

Grade 7–9

6 Why might using JPEG files cause a problem for a designer who regularly edits the same images more than once? [2]

Computer Networking

Wired and Wireless Networks 1

1 Describe what the abbreviations LAN and WAN stand for, and the relationship between them.

[4]

2 The Internet is described as the world's largest WAN, connecting LANs across the world.

State **two** connection methods for information to travel between countries. [2]

3 Circle which of the following modern devices commonly include network connectivity. [6]

Toaster   Smart TV   Smartphone   Vacuum cleaner

Internet radio   Games console   Tablet   Microwave

Media streamer   Audio amplifier   Desk lamp

4 Grace's Gadgets has a new office with a large LAN, but staff are puzzled as to why their network is so slow.

Describe **three** possible factors they should consider. [3]

5 Tariq has been using a peer-to-peer network for a while, but he is now concerned that some files are missing from his computer.

Why might this be the case? [2]

Computer Networking

Grade 7–9

6 Describe **two** advantages and **two** disadvantages of a client–server network. **[4]**

Wired and Wireless Networks 2

Grade 1–3

1 **a)** Describe **three** ways in which cloud computing would be beneficial to an international travel reporter. **[3]**

b) Using cloud technology, the travel reporter does find **one** problem while working away from home. What is it? **[1]**

Grade 4–6

2 Describe the difference between a switch and a router. **[2]**

Grade 4–6

3 Put the following transmission methods in order of potential distance of data travelled, with the shortest first. **[2]**

Fibre optic, Ethernet, Wi-Fi

Grade 4–6

4 If the Internet we know and use today is a vast interconnected collection of networks, then what is the World Wide Web? **[2]**

Computer Networking

Video Solution Question 2

5 What is a DNS and how does it help users browse the Internet? **[2]**

_____

_____

_____

Network Topologies

1 Draw diagrams to represent a star network topology and a mesh network topology. **[2]**

2 A nursery school wants to create a small network but cannot decide between a star and a mesh topology.

Provide **one** key advantage and **one** key disadvantage of each topology. **[4]**

_____

_____

_____

_____

_____

Computer Networking

Grade 4–6

3 What device, which is part of most network topologies, will cause the network to fail if it is damaged, and why? [2]

Grade 4–6

4 Why does a mesh network require more cabling than other topologies? [1]

Grade 7–9

5 Which network topology will not slow down by increasing the number of connected devices? [1]

Protocols and Layers

Grade 1–3

1 What does Gbps stand for? [1]

Grade 1–3

2 a) While visiting a fast-food restaurant, Jack receives a smartphone notification warning him about connecting to an open unsecure network.

Why should he be concerned? [3]

b) What should Jack look for when connecting to Wi-Fi networks? [2]

Computer Networking

3 An elderly couple setting up their first home computer and a mobile florist business have both set up their first email accounts.

Which email protocol might be the most appropriate for each, and why? **[4]**

4 Which protocol layer is primarily concerned with the communication of IP addresses between network routers? **[1]**

5 Describe how hardware and software standards might be applied to the design of a new laptop computer. **[4]**

System Security and Software

Common System Threats

Grade 1-3

1 Online shopping sites and social networks are often the focus of online attacks designed to steal personal information.

State **four** pieces of information that cyber-criminals would consider valuable. **[4]**

....

....

....

....

Grade 1-3

2 Match each term with its definition. **[2]**

Pharming		Installed by a user who thinks it is a legitimate piece of software when it is, in fact, malware.
Ransomware		The redirection from a user's website to a fraudulent site, by modifying their DNS entries.
Trojan		Limits or denies a user access to their system until a ransom is paid.

Grade 4-6

3 An anti-malware scan on an infected computer lists the presence of both a worm and a virus.

What is the difference between a worm and a virus? **[2]**

....

....

Grade 4-6

4 Describe how a phishing scam might allow a cyber-criminal to gain someone's bank details via telephone. **[3]**

....

....

....

System Security and Software

Grade 7–9

5 A controversial pop star has had their website closed by a DoS attack, and has been told that this will keep happening until a song is withdrawn.

Describe how this might have happened. [3]

Grade 7–9

6 A network policy informs members of an organisation about what they are and are not allowed to do when they are using on-site computers.

State **three** aspects of a user's work life that might be covered by this policy. [3]

Threat Prevention

Grade 1–3

1 Why must anti-malware be updated regularly? [2]

Grade 1–3

2 A social network would like users to improve their security settings, and it wants to provide a list of five top tips for creating a strong password.

State **five** pieces of advice the social network might offer in its list. [5]

System Security and Software

Grade 4–6

3 Describe **three** ways in which encryption can improve the security of an organisation's network. [3]

Grade 4–6

4 A hospital has been advised to set user access levels for the staff who use its computer network.

State **three** possible reasons for this advice. [3]

Grade 7–9

5 An organisation that is concerned about its online security hires an expert in penetration testing to try to access its system.

What will the expert be looking for during the penetration testing? [3]

Grade 7–9

6 Describe the difference between a public encryption key and a private encryption key. [2]

System Security and Software

System Software

Grade 1–3

1 Describe **two** user benefits of a graphical user interface. [2]

....

....

Grade 1–3

2 Match each term with its definition. [3]

Third-party applications		The process of reducing the file size of a computer file to use less disk space.

Utility software		The software link between the hardware, software and user.

Operating system		Performs specific tasks, for example security, to support the operating system.

Compression		Designed by an external organisation, often as an alternative software solution.

Grade 4–6

3 Describe the process of memory management within an operating system. [2]

....

....

....

Grade 4–6

4 A new webcam and microphone have been plugged into a home computer.

What will the operating system need to install or update before it can communicate with them? [1]

....

System Security and Software

5 Why might the following types of organisation need encryption software?

a) School [1]

_____

b) Games design company [1]

_____

c) Social network [1]

_____

d) Hospital [1]

_____

6 A small printing business has contacted a computer support consultant because their office machine is running slowly.

The consultant recommends using defragmentation utility software.

What is this and how does it work? [3]

_____

_____

_____

Ethical, Legal, Cultural and Environmental Concerns

Ethical and Legal Concerns

Grade 4–6

1 A government employee loses his smartphone when travelling for work. He needs to retrieve it because he is concerned about its contents.

Describe **three** systems that could be used to try to locate it. **[3]**

Grade 4–6

2 Judy joins a large social network and is surprised to find that all of the services it offers are free.

Explain how large social networks generate income. **[4]**

Grade 4–6

3 Governments around the world would like to monitor our digital footprint so that they can identify potentially dangerous threats.

Provide **three** examples of what the term 'digital footprint' refers to. **[3]**

Grade 4–6

4 Describe **three** examples of situations where automated devices can work in locations potentially dangerous to humans. **[3]**

Ethical, Legal, Cultural and Environmental Concerns

Grade 4–6

5 Describe how criminals are using the Internet to commit offences in the following areas.

a) Films and TV [1]

b) Banking [1]

c) Motor vehicles [1]

d) Illegal substances [1]

Grade 7–9

6 Ray is sharing a house at university. He receives a letter from his ISP saying he has been breaking copyright laws and his contract may be cancelled. He does not understand why this has happened.

State **two** possible reasons why this has happened. [2]

Cultural and Environmental Concerns

Grade 1–3

1 Briefly describe the term 'digital divide'. [2]

Grade 4–6

2 State an example of how computer technology might affect the life of a typical adult in each of the following situations.

a) Accessing local and international news at breakfast time [1]

b) Listening to music on the train to work [1]

c) Working as an estate agent [1]

d) Booking a holiday over lunch [1]

e) Talking to family during the evening [1]

f) Evening meal time [1]

g) Watching a movie [1]

h) Reading [1]

3 Explain how online tutorials and videos have changed the ways in which children and adults can learn new skills. [4]

Ethical, Legal, Cultural and Environmental Concerns

 4 Complete the following table on the positive and negatives impacts of technology on the environment. Add a tick in the 'positive' or 'negative' column for each, as appropriate. **[10]**

	Positive	Negative
Increased energy consumption of digital devices		
Increased greenhouse gas emissions to meet additional power needs		
Reductions in the amount of paper used		
Use of toxic materials in device manufacture		
Increasingly efficient renewable energy production systems		
Recycling waste materials from outdated or unwanted technology		
Downloads require fewer materials than physical media		
The transportation and use of raw and synthetic materials in the production of smart devices		
Impact on travel and commuting due to increased remote working		
Smart devices being able to control their energy usage		

Grade 4–6 **5** Briefly describe why the number of unwanted electrical devices is increasing faster than ever before. **[2]**

Grade 7–9 **6** How might technology help a surgeon to perform an operation from a remote location? **[2]**

Ethical, Legal, Cultural and Environmental Concerns

Computer Science Legislation

Grade 1–3

1 Match each piece of legislation with its definition. [2]

Data Protection Act 2018	To prevent the hacking and damaging of computer systems.
Computer Misuse Act 1990	To provide creators of media with the right to control how their products are accessed and sold.
Copyright, Designs and Patents Act 1988	To protect the personal information held about individuals within organisations.

Grade 4–6

2 What is meant by the term 'copyright'? [2]

....

....

....

....

Grade 4–6

3 Prabhat is a designer who wants to add high-quality photos to his promotional website. State **three** legal ways he might achieve this. [3]

....

....

....

4 Fiona is opening a cupcake business and has been advised to use open source software to save money.

What does the term 'open source' mean? [2]

5 State **four** principles of the Data Protection Act 2018. [4]

Algorithms and Computational Logic

Algorithms and Flowcharts

Grade 4–6

1 An amusement park ride program opens and closes an entry gate until the maximum number of people have got on the ride.

What type of algorithm is this? **[1]**

....

Grade 4–6

2 A programmer has been asked to create a virtual driving simulator.

How will abstraction help to design a solution? **[2]**

....

....

Grade 4–6

3 Draw the correct flowchart shape for the following functions: **[5]**

Start/stop	
Input/output	
Decision	
Process	
Sub-program/routine	

Algorithms and Computational Logic

Grade 4–6 **4** Explain the purpose of a 'structure diagram' when tackling a programming problem. **[2]**

Searching and Sorting Algorithms

Grade 4–6 **1** Match each type of sort to the correct description. **[2]**

| Bubble sort | Each item in an unordered list is examined in turn and compared with the previous items in the list. |

| Merge sort | Pairs of values in a list are compared to each other and swapped until they are in the correct order. |

| Insertion sort | Data is repeatedly split into halves until each list contains only one item. |

Grade 7–9 **2** Why must a data set be ordered when a binary search is carried out? **[3]**

Grade 7–9 **3** Carry out a bubble sort on the data set (6,2,4,1,8) to put the values in ascending order. **[5]**

Pseudocode 1

Grade 4–6 **1** What is the difference between pseudocode and a programming language such as Python? **[2]**

Algorithms and Computational Logic

2 State a pseudocode keyword that might be used in a program to provide a response
a) if a statement is met and **b)** if a statement is not met. **[2]**

3 Within an algorithm/program, what is the difference between a variable and a constant? **[3]**

4 A music streaming algorithm is being written by a team of developers. Why is the use of comments so important? **[2]**

5 Explain the term 'naming convention' and provide **two** common coding examples. **[4]**

6 Write a simple algorithm/program that is used to check the weight of luggage being put into the hold of a plane. If the value is greater than 30, then 'Too heavy' is displayed; otherwise, 'OK' is displayed. **[4]**

Algorithms and Computational Logic

Pseudocode 2

1 Which type of error is a simple typing mistake or use of the wrong character known as? **[1]**

2 Describe the purpose of the following short program. **[3]**

```
stepOne = input("Please enter your password")
stepTwo = input("Please confirm your password again")
if stepOne == stepTwo then
    print("Access granted")
else
    print("Access denied")
end
```

3 What does the following pseudocode do? **[3]**

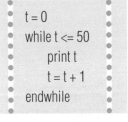

```
t = 0
while t <= 50
    print t
    t = t + 1
endwhile
```

4 Describe the difference between the operators MOD and DIV. **[2]**

Algorithms and Computational Logic

Grade 7–9

5 Write a simple algorithm/program that asks for the three dimensions required and then calculates and returns the volume of a room. **[5]**

Grade 7–9

6 Write a short algorithm/program that allows cheaper train tickets to be bought for children under 16 OR adults over 65. A cheap ticket costs £10; a standard ticket costs £20. **[3]**

Boolean Logic

Grade 4–6

1 Draw the standard shapes for an AND, OR and NOT gate. **[3]**

Algorithms and Computational Logic

Grade 4–6

2 The NOT gate is sometimes referred to as an inverter. Why is this?   **[1]**

_____

Grade 4–6

3 Identify **two** mistakes in the logic diagram below.   **[2]**

A ———⊐ C

B —o◁ ⊐ D

_____

Grade 4–6

4 Draw a truth table for a standard NOT gate.   **[4]**

Grade 7–9

5 Create a truth table for the following logic circuit.   **[5]**

A ——⊐ D
B ——⊐ K ▷o— Z

Grade 7–9

6 Draw a logic diagram and a truth table for the following:

A NOT gate connected to the output of an AND gate.   **[6]**

Programming Techniques, Programs, Translators and Languages

Programming Techniques 1

1 Nik's Shack, a mountain bike shop, is creating a database of stock bikes.

Complete the following table by selecting a suitable data type for each field.   **[5]**

Field	Example	Data type
bikeBrand	Peak Buster	
numberofGears	18	
overallWeight	10.4	
colourCode	S	
inStock	Yes	

2 What would the following pieces of pseudocode do?

a)   `int("1977")`   **[1]**

b)   `str(3827)`   **[1]**

3 What would be the best data type to use in the following scenarios?

a) The entry of an alphanumeric password   **[1]**

b) The precise weight of a metal   **[1]**

c) A Yes/No question about personal food preferences   **[1]**

d) Asking a user for their age in years   **[1]**

Grade 4–6

4 Explain the term 'concatenation' in relation to programming. [2]

Grade 7–9

5 Write a simple algorithm/program that does the following:

- asks for the first and last name of the user

- asks for the year of birth of the user

- takes the first letter of the first name, the first letter of the last name and the year of birth to generate a username, and returns this on screen. [4]

Grade 7–9

6 Consider a text file called 'story.txt'

Write a short algorithm/program to open the file and print the first line. [4]

Programming Techniques, Programs, Translators and Languages

Programming Techniques 2

1 State **three** reasons why a programmer may use sub-programs to improve the efficiency of a program. [3]

_____

_____

_____

2 Nik's Shack now has a database of mountain bikes in stock, which is called 'Stock'.

bikeID	bikeBrand	numberofGears	overallWeight	colourCode	inStock
0001	Peak Buster	18	10.4	S	Yes
0002	PB Wheelers	21	13.2	R	Yes
0003	Peak Buster	24	11.3	G	No
0004	Team PB	18	12.4	B	Yes
0005	PB Wheelers	24	14.3	Y	Yes

a) How many records does the database have? [1]

_____

b) How many fields does each record have? [1]

_____

c) What would be the problem with a single character colour code? [1]

_____

d) Which field is the primary key? _____ [1]

3 Still looking at Nik's Shack 'Stock' database, write SQL queries in order to:

a) list all of the bikes with the colour code 'G'. [1]

_____

b) search for all bikes that have more than 20 gears. [1]

_____

c) search for bikes that have 18 gears AND are in stock. [1]

_____

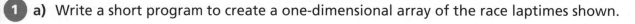

Programming Techniques 3

1 **a)** Write a short program to create a one-dimensional array of the race laptimes shown. **[2]**

	0	1	2	3
Laptime	59.4	64.3	74.3	81.9

b) How might this be turned into a two-dimensional array? **[1]**

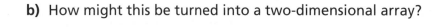

2 Sub-programs can contain both parameters and arguments.

Describe the difference between these. **[2]**

3 Oscar is writing a weather application and will be using multiple sub-programs.

a) Write a short sub-program to carry out a conversion from Celsius (C) to Fahrenheit (F) when required. **[4]**

Note: $F = (C \times 1.8) + 32$

b) Why is Oscar using a function rather than a procedure? **[1]**

Programming Techniques, Programs, Translators and Languages

Producing Robust Programs

1 Testing data is an essential part of the design process. Match each term with its definition. **[3]**

Normal data

Values of the correct data type but that cannot be processed as they are outside pre-determined limits.

Boundary data

Incorrect data of a type that should be rejected by the program or system.

Invalid data

Acceptable, error-free data likely to be input into the program.

Erroneous data

Values at the limit of what a program should be able to accept, minimum and maximum dates for example.

2 Daisy is writing a program to be used in a school classroom. A friend has reminded her to consider defensive design when designing a system to be used by children.

a) What is defensive design? **[2]**

....

....

b) Describe **three** ways in which this can be applied to a system to be used by children. **[3]**

....

....

....

....

3 Andrew is just starting out as a programmer and a colleague provides him with a list of tips to keep his programs well maintained.

Describe **four** tips for good program maintenance. **[4]**

....

....

....

....

....

Programming Techniques, Programs, Translators and Languages

Grade 4–6 **4** When checking through a first version of an address book program, Rachel finds several syntax and logic errors.

What are the differences between these two types of error? **[2]**

....

....

Grade 4–6 **5** Logic errors are often more difficult to solve. Why might this be the case? **[2]**

....

....

Grade 7–9 **6** Pawel is carrying out a range of tests on a computer-based version of a popular board game.

How does boundary and erroneous data differ to normal data? **[2]**

....

....

Languages, Translators and Integrated Development Environment

Grade 4–6 **1** Isaac has been asked to choose a high-level programming language to focus on during a university course.

List at least **four** current high-level programming languages open to him. **[4]**

....

....

....

....

Grade 4–6 **2** Many programmers still specialise in using low-level languages.

State **two** reasons why this might be the case. **[2]**

....

....

Programming Techniques, Programs, Translators and Languages

3 Noah has written a financial application using an integrated development environment, and the code editor function has helped him to identify syntax errors.

Describe **two** ways this might have happened. [2]

....

....

4 State **three** ways in which an IDE helps a programmer to spot and rectify logic errors. [3]

....

....

....

5 Match each IDE functionality with its description. [3]

Editors	These will compile or interpret the final code as required.
Error diagnostics	This allows programs to be run virtually within the IDE software.
Run-time environment	Also known as debugging tools, these will help to identify errors in particular lines of code.
Translators	These are designed for writing source code, with tools to assist with formatting and syntax.

6 Having chosen a high-level programming language and written his first program, Isaac must now convert his work to machine code using a translator.

Identify **two** types of translator that can achieve this and the process involved. [4]

....

....

....

Collins

GCSE Computer Science
Paper 1: Computer Systems

Time allowed: 1 hour 30 minutes

Instructions

- Use black ink.
- Answer **all** the questions.
- Write your answer to each question in the spaces provided.
- You may **not** use a calculator.

Information

- The total mark for this paper is **80**.
- The marks for questions are shown in brackets **[ ]**.
- Quality of extended responses will be assessed in this paper in questions marked with an *.

Name: ....

1 Elizabeth is a freelance journalist with her own blog. She posts articles, images and videos from all over the UK, but finds that her smartphone and digital camera quickly run out of storage space.

(a) One of the new cameras she is considering has an option to upload images to the 'cloud'.

Explain what is meant by 'cloud storage'.

[1]

(b) Uploading files to the cloud brings advantages and disadvantages.

(i) Describe **two** advantages of storing files online.

[2]

(ii) Describe **two** disadvantages of storing files online.

[2]

(c) Elizabeth is considering upgrading the primary and secondary storage on her desktop computer.

Describe the difference between 'primary storage' and 'secondary storage' and provide an example of each.

[4]

2 Javed has a gaming PC that he built himself. In recent months, he is finding that the PC has become slower and new games are not running well. His first thought is to check the operating system is up to date.

(a) State **two** reasons why operating systems are regularly updated.

_____

_____ **[2]**

(b) Javed's friend recommends that he upgrade the RAM in his computer.

(i) Define the term 'RAM'.

_____

_____ **[1]**

(ii) Explain why having more RAM should improve the performance of a computer.

_____

_____ **[2]**

(c) Having done some research, Javed decides to try to reconfigure his operating system before he upgrades the hardware. He experiments with virtual memory settings and disk defragmentation.

(i) Define the term 'virtual memory'.

_____

_____ **[1]**

(ii) State **one** advantage and **one** disadvantage of using virtual memory.

_____

_____ **[2]**

(iii) Explain the process of disk defragmentation.

_____

_____ **[2]**

3 A cycle-hire business, specialising in electric bikes, has expanded to a second shop in a woodland area. The business owners make use of computers and tablet devices for bookings, and they need to make sure that they have a reliable system in place.

(a) Devices in the shop are connected to a LAN.

　(i) Define the term 'LAN'.

　　..

　　.. **[1]**

　(ii) The business connects its LAN to a second LAN in the other shop. State the device needed to connect them together, and what could be created as a result?

　　..

　　.. **[2]**

(b) Wireless technology is used in the shop and the owners are concerned about its security and which encryption option to use.

　(i) State **three** common wireless encryption standards.

　　..

　　..

　　.. **[3]**

　(ii) Explain which standard they should use and why.

　　..

　　.. **[2]**

(c) The shop also has a children's seating area with tablet computers for children to play cycle games and look at videos while parents make bookings. These devices were designed to meet modern hardware and software standards.

　Why are hardware and software standards important for modern devices?

　..

　.. **[2]**

4   An independent film production company specialises in creating film shorts on a budget that look like more expensive productions. All of their films are shot and edited digitally, and the company is constantly looking for new software and media clips it can use.

(a) State which legislative Act applies to the following aspects of their business.

   (i) Concerns about their films being pirated and shared online before official release.

   _____ [1]

   (ii) Making sure the personal details of all employees and customers are secure.

   _____ [1]

(b) When editing film and music tracks, the company can save their files in either lossy or lossless format.

   (i) Explain the difference between the two formats.

   _____

   _____ [2]

   (ii) State which format would be the more appropriate when editing content and explain why this would be the case.

   _____

   _____ [2]

(c) Live bands are often brought in to the editing studio to create a high-quality original recording.

   State the name of the process of transferring analogue to digital audio and explain the importance of sample rate and bit depth.

   _____

   _____

   _____

   _____ [3]

5   Ian runs a small computer consultancy company, offering advice on infrastructure, networks and security.

(a) Two of the services that Ian offers are penetration testing and advice on user access levels.

    (i) Define the term 'penetration testing'.

    ....

    .... **[1]**

    (ii) Define the term 'user access levels'.

    ....

    .... **[1]**

(b) Many of the organisations he works with dispose of unwanted, but still serviceable, equipment straight to landfill.

    (i) State **three** reasons for **not** doing this.

    ....

    ....

    .... **[3]**

    (ii) State an ethical alternative to disposing of unwanted equipment.

    ....

    .... **[1]**

6   A world news organisation is expanding its website to include a subscription service that will pay for additional journalists around the world. The organisation is very concerned with security, as an older version of its website was often attacked.

(a) The original website was the victim of a DoS attack. Define the term 'DoS attack'.

....

.... **[1]**

(b) Subscription customers are reminded to create a strong password when setting up their account.

State **three** pieces of password advice.

....

....

.... **[3]**

(c) The subscription page of the site is a HTTPS page.

(i) Define the term 'HTTPS'.

....

.... **[1]**

(ii) HTTPS is a network protocol. Explain what is meant by a network protocol.

....

.... **[1]**

(d) Customers of the original website were often targeted by malware.

State **three** different pieces of malware and explain the damage each can cause.

....

....

....

....

....

....

_____

_____

_____

_____

_____

_____

_____ [6]

7 Alexander is setting up a client–server network. It will serve multiple workstations in a computer-based training room. He has narrowed it down to three choices; see **Fig. 1.**

Fig. 1

Server 1	Server 2	Server 3
CPU Clock Speed: 3.2 GHz	CPU Clock Speed: 2.4 GHz	CPU Clock Speed: 2.8 GHz
CPU Cores: 2	CPU Cores: 1	CPU Cores: 4
Hard Drive Space: 500 GB	Hard Drive Space: 750 GB	Hard Drive Space: 1 TB

(a) Identify the most appropriate server and give **two** reasons for your choice.

_____

_____

_____ [3]

(b) A star network topology has been chosen.

Describe **two** advantages and **two** disadvantages of using this network topology.

_____

_____

_____

_____ [4]

(c) Explain **three** benefits a network manager will get from using client–server-linked workstations rather than individual computers.

....

....

....

....

....

....

.... **[3]**

8   A university has designed an e-learning platform that can be installed on all devices across the campus.

(a) Students have requested that all messages are encrypted.

Define the term 'encryption'.

....

.... **[2]**

(b) Students are also concerned about social engineering.

(i) Define the term 'social engineering'.

....

.... **[1]**

(ii) Describe **three** examples of how it can take place.

....

....

.... **[3]**

9* An international bank is improving its network and security systems across the world. This is in response to concerns about both the online and physical security of the financial data it holds.

Many people are concerned that it is impossible to protect data from theft.

Discuss this statement, considering potential solutions.

[8]

Collins

GCSE Computer Science
Paper 2: Computational Thinking, Algorithms and Programming

Time allowed: 1 hour 30 minutes

Instructions

- Use black ink.
- Answer **all** the questions.
- Write your answer to each question in the spaces provided.
- You may **not** use a calculator.

Information

- The total mark for this paper is **80**.
- The marks for questions are shown in brackets **[ ]**.

Name: ....

SECTION A

1 Finn manages an electric car showroom and has a database of regular customers. The database is called VipCustomers; see **Fig. 1**.

Fig. 1

custID	surname	firstName	carsBought	houseNumber	postCode	contactNumber
0001	Peak	Ray	3	161	VC1 4RD	07123827645
0002	Peak	Judy	2	9	VC2 7YT	01293837645
0003	Ibex	Rob	4	32	VC7 3EK	01293695641
0004	Ibex	Katie	1	4	VC2 4RD	07256453726

(a) Describe the difference between a record and a field.

....

.... **[2]**

(b) Create database searches using Structured Query Language (SQL) to display the following.

(i) All the records of customers who have bought only one car.

....

.... **[1]**

(ii) The first name of customers who have bought three or more cars.

....

.... **[1]**

(iii) The first name, surname and contact number of customers from the VC2 4RD postcode.

....

....

.... **[1]**

2   Consider the following data sequence: 13, 32, 10, 19

(a) Show the stages of a bubble sort when applied to this sequence.

[3]

(b) Describe the process of carrying out a linear search on the same sequence to find the value 10.

[3]

(c) A linear search is inefficient for large datasets.

State the type of search that should be used for large datasets.

[1]

3   Catherine manages a netball team and is building a program to record the goals scored. **Fig. 2**, titled goalsScored, shows the player numbers of three team members and the number of goals they have scored.

Fig. 2

	0	1	2	3
0	12	3	3	2
1	13	2	4	5
2	14	6	4	7

(a) It has been recommended that Catherine should use an array.

(i) Write an algorithm to create this table as a two-dimensional array.

....

....

....

....

.... **[3]**

(ii) Write a short search algorithm to return the number of goals scored by player
number 13 in their third game.

....

.... **[1]**

(b) In respect to the amount of data it can store, state how a one-dimensional array
differs from a two-dimensional array.

....

.... **[1]**

4   Consider a two-level logic circuit with three inputs, A, B and C, and an output, X.

(a) Create a logic circuit diagram that represents the Boolean expression:

   (i) X = (A OR B) AND (NOT C).

[3]

(ii) Complete the following truth table for the same expression.

A	B	C	X

[8]

(b) Describe the purpose of the following logic circuit.

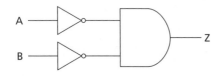

....

....

[2]

5   Noah is part of a development team that writes smartwatch applications.
He specialises in small graphical and audio elements. A graphical icon has the
hexadecimal code: 69 96

(a) Convert the hexadecimal code into a series of binary numbers and complete the
table below to show the icon. Use 0 = White and 1 = Black.

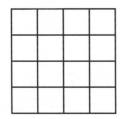

[5]

(b) The application is limited to a 4-bit image.

State how many colours this would allow.

....[1]

(c) File compression is used to save all images used in the application.

Describe **one** advantage and **one** disadvantage of this method.

_____

_____

_____

_____
                                                                    [2]

6 **(a)** Insert the missing unit in this ordered list of data storage sizes.

    MB   GB   __   PB   **[1]**

(b) Convert the decimal number 249 into an 8-bit binary number.

_____
                                                                    [1]

(c) Trying to convert the number 259 into an 8-bit binary number results in an overflow.

Define the term 'overflow' in this context.

_____

_____
                                                                    [1]

(d) Add the following binary numbers together and give the answer as a binary and a decimal number:

10010010

00001100

_____
                                                                    [2]

(e) Convert the hexadecimal number E9 into a decimal number and show your working.

_____

_____
                                                                    [2]

7   A UK mobile telephone number in the format 07######### will often need to be written in the international format +447#########.

(a) Write an algorithm that asks for a UK mobile number, replaces the first 0 with the prefix +44 and returns the result to the user. It should also return 'not recognised' for numbers not starting with a '0'.

[5]

(b) The international UK number begins with the + symbol.

State the most suitable data type for handling this symbol.

[1]

SECTION B

Some questions require you to respond using either an exam-style reference language or a high-level programming language. These will be clearly labelled.

8   Emelia is developing a range of small applications to be built into a child-friendly tablet computer.

   (a) Her first program (see **Fig. 3**) simulates two dice being rolled to start a board game. The program makes use of the random function and the numbers on both dice need to match for the game to start. If not, they are rolled again.

Fig. 3

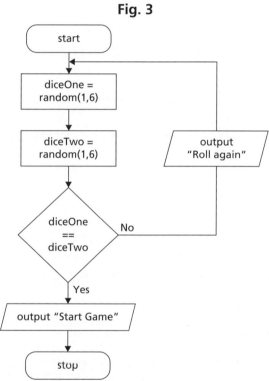

   (i) State **two** variables in the program.

   ....

   .... **[2]**

   (ii) Explain the process taking place within the diamond shape.

   ....

   .... **[2]**

(b) In order to process dice roll outcomes, the data needs to be stored.

What data type would be the most appropriate for the results of a dice roll?
Tick **one** box and explain your choice.

Data Type	Tick one box
String	
Integer	
Real	
Boolean	

Explanation: _____

_____ **[2]**

(c) Emelia would now like to write this as a sub-program.

   (i) Describe whether this program would be a function or a procedure and explain your choice.

_____

_____ **[2]**

   (ii) Write a short program representing the flowchart as a sub-program.
    *You must use **either**:*

-    *an exam-style reference language **or***
-    *a high-level programming language you are studying.*

[4]

(d) Complete the test plan below for the flowchart in **Fig 3**.

Test Data	Test Type	Expected Result
diceOne = 2 diceTwo = 3	Normal	Roll again
diceOne = 1 diceTwo = 6	Boundary	
diceOne = 9 diceTwo = 7		
diceOne = 4 diceTwo = 4		

[5]

(e) Emelia's next program is a child-friendly weather application. Part of the program converts Celsius into Fahrenheit. Users are asked to enter a temperature in Celsius; a calculation is carried out and the value is returned to them in Fahrenheit.

```
tempC = input("Please enter the temperature in Celsius")
tempF = tempC * 1.8
tempF = tempF + 32
print (tempF)
```

(i) Complete the trace table below using an input value of 10 degrees Celsius.

Line	Input (TempC)	tempF	Output
1			
2			
3			
4			

[4]

(ii) The program is being refined to also display whether the current temperature in Fahrenheit is above or below the average temperature for the time of year. The average is represented by the variable 'averageTemp'. Improve the original program to include this functionality.

*You must use **either**:*

- *an exam-style reference language **or***

- *a high-level programming language you are studying.*

[4]

(f) Emelia has also been asked to add a feature that checks how long the user has been using the tablet. It displays a warning if it is over the three-hour limit on any one day.

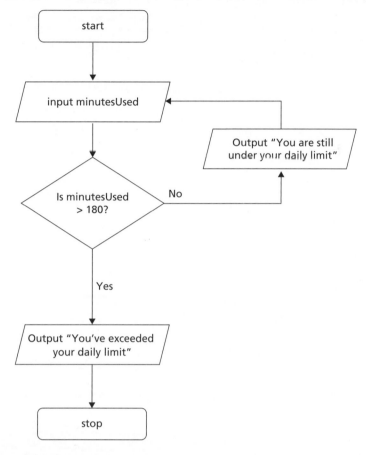

Rewrite the flowchart as a program.

*You must use **either**:*

- *an exam-style reference language **or***

- *a high-level programming language you are studying.*

....

....

....

....

....

....

.... **[4]**

Notes

Answers

The Purpose and Function of the Central Processing Unit

1.

Input	A device that sends information or data to the CPU.
Output	A device that receives instructions or data from the CPU.
Software	Programmed instructions for a computer with a specific task.
Hardware	Any physical device that would normally form part of a computer system.

[3]

2.

[3]

3. Memory [1]

4. Stored program means that both the computer program and the data it processes are stored in memory [2]

5. The arithmetic logic unit (ALU) is where calculations and logic comparisons are carried out, and the results of these calculations and logic comparisons are stored in the accumulator until they are needed [2]

6. The control unit [1]

Systems Architecture

1. Clock speed is the rate at which instructions are processed by the CPU per second [1]

2. The whole system may still function if a non-essential embedded system is damaged [1]. Different manufacturers can simultaneously work on embedded systems during production [1]

3. Multicore processors have more than one CPU on the same chip [1]; this means that tasks can be carried out simultaneously, which speeds up the system [1]

4. Any **four** of the following:
An instruction is fetched from memory [1]
The instruction is then decoded [1]
The decoded instruction is then executed so that the CPU performs continuously [1]
The process is repeated [1]
The program counter is incremented [1]
The instruction is transferred to the MDR [1]
The address of the instruction to be fetched is placed in the MAR [1]

5. Accept either of the following:
L1 cache is smaller [1], but faster [1].
L2 cache is larger [1], but slower [1].

6. Embedded systems are often installed deep into the machine [1] and if they fail can be difficult to replace or repair [1].

Memory

1. RAM is a temporary area that a computer uses to store data in current use [1]

2. a) Volatile means that once power is switched off, all stored data is lost [1]. Non-volatile means that any instructions written are permanently kept without power [1].
b) Manufacturers can write instructions to ROM, such as BIOS, and these cannot be changed or edited [1]

3. The main memory component of a computer system [1]

4. True [1]

5. a) Basic input/output system [1]
b) It ensures hardware communications [1]; it starts running the operating system [1]

6. a) It is created because the RAM becomes full [1]
b) It is created on the hard drive [1]
c) As secondary storage communication is not as fast as RAM, the system will become slow if secondary storage communication is used too much [1]

Storage Types, Devices and Characteristics

1. Magnetic storage is large [1] and has complex moving parts that could be damaged with physical use [1]

2. Any five of the following: capacity [1]; speed [1]; portability [1]; durability [1]; reliability [1]; cost [1]

3. a) CD [1]; DVD [1]; Blu-ray [1]
b) Discs can be damaged easily [1]; capacity is limited by type [1]; the correct writer/player must be used [1]

4. The original device has more storage capacity [1], but the new device will run faster [1]

5. Any **two** of the following: An optical drive is slower to access than others [1], is liable to skip/jump if it is moved [1] and has limited capacity [1]

6. At regular intervals, move the stored files to a new storage media technology [1]

Units and Formats of Data

1.

high-definition video	gigabytes
MP3 audio file	megabytes
system backup files	terabytes
word processing document	kilobytes

[3]

2. a) 156 [1]
b) 246 [1]
c) 75 [1]
d) 33 [1]

Answers

3. Character or coding groups **[1]**
4. Unicode **[1]**
5. To provide capacity to represent another 128 characters **[1]**; to allow it to be used with common 8-bit systems **[1]**
6. Examples: Backspace **[1]**; Enter (Carriage return) **[1]**; Escape **[1]**; Tab **[1]**

Converting Data 1
1. a) 00010010 **[1]**
   b) 00011001 **[1]**
   c) 11111011 **[1]**
   d) 10100001 **[1]**
2. a) 11101010 **[1]** 234 **[1]**
   b) 01011001 **[1]** 89 **[1]**
3. Example: 11111100 + 10000000 (380) **[1]**
4. a) 01101010 **[1]**
   b) 01001100 **[1]**
5. a) 01101010 **[1]**
   b) 00101101 **[1]**
6. To carry out multiplication and division **[1]**

Converting Data 2
1. a) FE **[1]**
   b) 63 **[1]**
   c) 2A **[1]**
2. 42 49 47 **[3]**
3. a) 79 **[1]**
   b) 140 **[1]**
   c) 18 **[1]**
4. Because long binary sequences can be shortened to a more manageable hexadecimal sequence **[1]**
5. They might see it as the denary number 24 rather than the characters 2 and 4 **[1]**
6. It is a shortcut reference **[1]** language, created by programmers **[1]**

Audio/Visual Formats and Compression
1. a) 1 bit **[1]**
   b) 2 bits **[1]**
   c) 4 bits **[1]**
2. To catalogue data by (any two of): location **[1]**; date **[1]**; time **[1]**; camera settings **[1]**
3. RAW is a lossless file format, so all the original image data is maintained **[1]**
4. MP3 **[1]**, because the small file size is easy to download **[1]**, and the quality can be adjusted to suit user requirements **[1]**
5. Benefit: high-quality accurate recording **[1]**; drawback: large digital file size **[1]**
6. The file type JPEG uses lossy compression **[1]**, so each time the file is saved, more data is lost **[1]**

Pages 159–163 Computer Networking

Wired and Wireless Networks 1
1. Local area network (LAN) **[1]**; wide area network (WAN) **[1]**. A WAN is formed by connecting two or more LANs together **[1]** across large distances **[1]**
2. Fibre-optic cables **[1]**; satellites **[1]**
3. Smart TV **[1]**; smartphone **[1]**; Internet radio **[1]**; games console **[1]**; tablet **[1]**; media streamer **[1]**

4. Network bandwidth **[1]**; interference from external factors and devices **[1]**; the number of users connecting at the same time **[1]**
5. He may have not checked the permission settings of the network **[1]** and so other users have been allowed access to his files **[1]**
6. Advantages: software and security settings are controlled centrally **[1]**; client computers can be of relatively low specification **[1]**. Disadvantages: if the server fails, so does the network **[1]**; low-specification client machines can run quite slowly **[1]**

Wired and Wireless Networks 2
1. a) Files can be saved and accessed anywhere **[1]**; word processing and image editing software can be accessed via a browser **[1]**; storage devices do not need to be carried **[1]**
   b) Without an Internet connection, cloud services cannot be accessed **[1]**
2. A switch connects network compatible devices together on the same network **[1]**, whereas a router connects different networks together **[1]**
3. Shortest first: Wi-Fi, Ethernet, fibre optic **[2]**
4. A system to publish linked pages written in HTML **[1]** that can be viewed using a web browser anywhere in the world **[1]**
5. Domain Name Service (or Servers) **[1]** is an Internet naming service that links the IP address of a computer on a network to a text-based website address that is easier to remember **[1]**

Network Topologies
1.
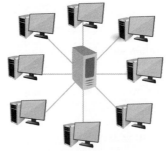

Star Topology

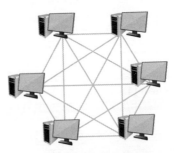

Mesh Topology **[2]**

2. Any of the following:
   Star advantages: the failure of a device, as long as it is not the server, will not halt the network **[1]**; the network can be expanded by adding devices **[1]**; localised problems can be identified quickly **[1]**; data can be directed to a specific address via the central server **[1]**

Answers

Star disadvantages: if the server fails, the whole network will collapse [1]; extensive cabling and technical knowledge is needed to maintain the server [1]
Mesh advantages: all devices share the network load [1]; if a device fails, the network will continue to run [1]; adding more devices will not affect the speed of the network [1]
Mesh disadvantages: managing the network requires a high level of network expertise [1]; it can be expensive to set up because of the number of devices required [1]
3. The server [1]. It directs the flow of data between devices [1].
4. Every device in the network needs to be connected to every other device in the network [1]
5. Mesh [1]

Protocols and Layers
1. Gigabits per second [1]
2. a) An open unsecure network can be connected to by any device [1]; these devices may pass malware onto the network [1] and can potentially steal personal information [1]
   b) An encrypted network connection [1] using WPA, WPA2 or WPA3 [1]
3. Elderly couple: Post Office Protocol [1], as all emails are downloaded to their home [1]. Florist: IMAP [1], as emails can be synced at home and on mobile devices on the move [1]
4. Internet (or Network) layer [1]
5. Hardware standards allow components from different manufacturers to be connected [1] and to be connected to the Internet [1]. Software standards allow applications to be installed on common operating systems [1] and use common file types [1].

Pages 164–168 **System Security and Software**

Common System Threats
1. Any four of the following: usernames [1]; passwords [1]; bank account numbers [1]; personal email addresses [1]; answers to secret questions [1]; full names [1]
2.

Pharming	The redirection from a user's website to a fraudulent site, by modifying their DNS entries.
Ransomware	Limits or denies a user access to their system until a ransom is paid.
Trojan	Installed by a user who thinks it is a legitimate piece of software when it is, in fact, malware.

[2]

3. A virus must be transferred from one computer to another via another file [1], for example an email attachment, whereas a worm can replicate itself between systems [1]

4. Telephone a member of the public, pretending to be their bank [1], ask them to confirm and obtain their bank details following a fictitious security problem [1], and then use these to commit a crime [1]
5. The website was flooded with false data traffic [1], causing the server to crash [1], and this will be repeated until the song is withdrawn [1]
6. The transfer of files to and from the workplace [1]; Internet browsing rules [1]; the use of personal devices in the workplace [1]

Threat Prevention
1. As new virus codes appear every day [1], anti-malware software must be updated to include the latest patches [1]
2. Any five of the following: make sure they are at least eight characters long [1]; use upper- and lower-case characters [1]; include special characters [1]; avoid real dictionary words [1]; avoid any personal information [1]; regularly change any password [1]
3. Encrypted files can be stored safely [1], with no external access from unwanted users [1], and intercepted messages cannot be read [1]
4. Ensuring that staff cannot access personal information [1]; making sure that any sensitive data cannot be removed from the network [1]; making sure that external devices, which potentially carry viruses, cannot be used [1]
5. Any three of the following: weak passwords [1]; previously unknown access methods [1]; system areas vulnerable to virus attack [1]; potential SQL injection areas [1]
6. A public key is known by all and is a method used to encrypt a message [1], but the private key needed to decrypt the message is known only to the recipient of the message [1].

System Software
1. Users do not have to use command prompt text functions [1] and users can visually drag and drop files [1].
2.

Third-party applications	Designed by an external organisation, often as an alternative software solution.
Utility software	Performs specific tasks, for example security, to support the operating system.
Operating system	The software link between the hardware, software and user.
Compression	The process of reducing the file size of a computer file to use less disk space.

[3]

Answers

3. The managing and allocating of free space and prioritising the amount of memory [1] and resources that the CPU and memory modules can use [1]
4. Device drivers [1]
5. a) To keep students' personal details private [1]
   b) To protect unreleased games from being accessed and stolen [1]
   c) To keep the usernames and passwords secure [1]
   d) To protect the medical records of patients [1]
6. Defragmentation utility software analyses data and how it is stored on a disk [1]. It then rearranges files into a more logical sequence [1] to allow faster access [1]

Pages 169–174 Ethical, Legal, Cultural and Environmental Concerns

Ethical and Legal Concerns

1. Any three from: Triangulation using the mobile phone network [1]; GPS [1]; connection to Wi-Fi networks [1]; operating system or service provider 'lost phone' applications [1]
2. Organisations pay the social network to place advertising on the network [1]. Users' browsing habits on the network are tracked [1] and advertising is targeted at them [1] based on what they like and what their friends like [1]
3. Any three of the following: records of the websites we visit [1], the contents of instant messages/emails [1], the people we communicate with [1] and the locations of the devices we use [1]
4. Examples: scientific studies of a volcano [1]; bomb disposal [1]; deep underwater or space exploration [1]; nuclear or related power generation [1]
5. a) Sharing illegally obtained copies of new films/TV shows online [1]
   b) Stealing login details and transferring money to their own accounts [1]
   c) Selling cars through online auction sites without official paperwork [1]
   d) Selling drugs via online auction/dark websites without medical knowledge [1]
6. Examples: Someone in his household may have done two of the following: used a peer-to-peer network to download films/TV shows [1]; downloaded MP3s from an unofficial website [1]; shared with friends links to websites illegally offering films/TV shows [1]; or someone nearby may be accessing their Wi-Fi without permission [1]

Cultural and Environmental Concerns

1. The digital divide is the social and economic gap [1] between those who have and those who do not have access to computer technology [1]
2. Examples:
   a) Watching news on a laptop via streaming site or listening to news via a smartphone radio app [1]
   b) Using a music streaming app/using wireless headphones [1]
   c) Placing advertisements around the world/receiving photos and text via email [1]
   d) Browsing destinations/watching video reviews/using comparison sites [1]
   e) Using video chat to talk to relatives [1]
   f) Ordering a takeaway online or using an online recipe book [1]
   g) Downloading or streaming a film/booking cinema tickets online [1]
   h) Using an e-reader or reading a physical book that was ordered online [1]
3. Examples: Learning material can be accessed at any time [1] and in any place with an Internet connection [1]; material can be accessed that covers just about any topic [1] and it can be followed at the learners' own pace [1]
4.

	Positive	Negative
Increased energy consumption of digital devices		✓
Increased greenhouse gas emissions to meet additional power needs		✓
Reductions in the amount of paper used	✓	
Use of toxic materials in device manufacture		✓
Increasingly efficient renewable energy production systems	✓	
Recycling waste materials from outdated or unwanted technology	✓	
Downloads require fewer materials than physical media	✓	
The transportation and use of raw and synthetic materials in the production of smart devices		✓
Impact on travel and commuting due to increased remote working	✓	
Smart devices being able to control their energy usage	✓	

[10]

5. Users want the latest technology [1] before current technology comes to the end of its natural life [1]
6. Robotic/virtual technology could mimic the movements of the surgeon [1] across the Internet and recreate it at the patient's location [1]

Answers

Computer Science Legislation

1.

Data Protection Act 2018	To protect the personal information held about individuals within organisations.
Computer Misuse Act 1990	To prevent the hacking and damaging of computer systems.
Copyright, Designs and Patents Act 1988	To provide creators of media with the right to control how their products are accessed and sold.

[2]

2. Copyright is the legal right of the creators of music, books, films and games **[1]** to control how their products are accessed and sold **[1]**
3. Any three of the following: Take the photos himself **[1]**; purchase royalty-free images online **[1]**; download photos from a website that provides free images for commercial use **[1]**; seek permission to use copyrighted material **[1]**
4. Open source software can be freely downloaded and shared online **[1]**, with no limitations on its use **[1]**
5. Any four of the following:
   - Data should be used fairly, lawfully and transparently. **[1]**
   - Data must be obtained and used only for specified purposes. **[1]**
   - Data shall be adequate, relevant and not excessive. **[1]**
   - Data should be accurate and kept up to date. **[1]**
   - Data should not be kept for longer than necessary. **[1]**
   - Data must be kept safe and secure. **[1]**
   - Those organisations working with our data are accountable for all data protection and must produce evidence of their compliance. **[1]**

Pages 175–180 Algorithms and Computational Logic

Algorithms and Flowcharts

1. Iteration **[1]**
2. Abstraction is the removal of unnecessary information **[1]**; focusing on the car and the road rather than on the surroundings will help to create a solution **[1]**

3.

Start/stop		**[1]**
Input/output		**[1]**
Decision		**[1]**
Process		**[1]**
Sub-program / routine		**[1]**

4. A structure diagram is used to break down a problem into smaller problems **[1]**; each problem can also be broken down into sub-levels **[1]**

Searching and Sorting Algorithms

1.

Bubble sort	Pairs of values in a list are compared to each other and swapped until they are in the correct order.
Merge sort	Data is repeatedly split into halves until each list contains only one item.
Insertion sort	Each item in an unordered list is examined in turn and compared with the previous items in the list.

[2]

2. A binary search starts at the middle value **[1]**, then splits the data set **[1]** according to whether the data sought is above or below the middle value **[1]**
3. Five steps:
(6,2,4,1,8) to (2,6,4,1,8)	**[1]**
(2,6,4,1,8) to (2,4,6,1,8)	**[1]**
(2,4,6,1,8) to (2,4,1,6,8)	**[1]**
(2,4,1,6,8) to (2,1,4,6,8)	**[1]**
(2,1,4,6,8) to (1,2,4,6,8)	**[1]**

Pseudocode 1

1. Pseudocode is not a real programming language designed to run on a computer **[1]**, so mistakes and plain English terms do not prevent it from being understood **[1]**
2. a) then **[1]**; b) else **[1]**
3. The value stored in a variable can be changed while the program is running **[1]** but a constant cannot **[1]**. A constant value is assigned in the program code **[1]**.

Answers

4. Without comments, it might be difficult for the developers to understand the reasons for each other's coding choices **[1]**; the developers can leave messages within the code to help each other **[1]**
5. A naming convention refers to the naming of variables with a simple rule **[1]** and keeping that rule applied throughout all similar programs **[1]**
   Examples: using two words to define a variable but removing the space and using a capital letter on the second **[1]**, for example engineSize or fuelTank **[1]**
6. Example:

```
input weight                        [1]
if weight <= 30                     [1]
    print 'OK'                      [1]
else                                [1]
    print 'Too heavy'
end
```

Pseudocode 2

1. Syntax error **[1]**
2. A password is asked for twice **[1]**: if the two passwords match exactly **[1]** then access is granted, and if they do not match then access is not granted **[1]**
3. Counts **[1]** and prints **[1]** numbers from zero up to and including 50 **[1]**
4. MOD returns the remainder after a division **[1]**, while DIV divides but returns only a whole number (also known as an integer) **[1]**
5. Example:

```
length = input("what is the length of the room?")   [1]
width = input("what is the width of the room?")     [1]
height = input("what is the height of the room?")   [1]
roomVol = length * width * height                   [1]
print roomVol                                       [1]
end
```

6. Example:

```
age = input("How old are you?")          [1]
if age < 16 OR age > 65 then
    price = 10                           [1]
else
    price = 20
print ("The ticket cost is: £", price)   [1]
end
```

Boolean Logic

1. AND Gate

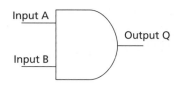

OR Gate

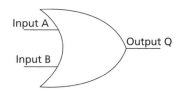

NOT Gate

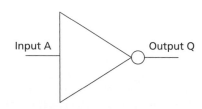

[3]

2. The NOT gate inverts the signal, so a 0 input becomes a 1 output and vice versa **[1]**
3. The NOT gate is reversed **[1]** and the AND gate has two outputs instead of one **[1]**
4.

Input	Output
A	**Q**
0	1
1	0

[4]

5.

A	B	D	K	Z	
0	0	0	0	1	**[1]**
0	1	1	1	0	**[1]**
1	0	1	0	1	**[1]**
1	1	1	1	0	**[1]**

First header row: **[1]**

6.

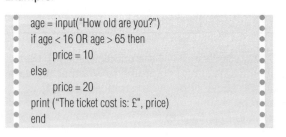

[2]

Inputs		Output
A	**B**	**C**
0	0	1
0	1	1
1	0	1
1	1	0

[4]

Answers

Programming Techniques 1

1.

Field	Example	Datatype
bikeBrand	Peak Buster	String
numberofGears	18	Integer
overallWeight	10.4	Real
colourCode	S	Character
inStock	Yes	Boolean

[5]

2. a) This converts the string 1977 to an integer **[1]**
   b) This converts the number 3827 to a string **[1]**
3. a) String **[1]**
   b) Real **[1]**
   c) Boolean **[1]**
   d) Integer **[1]**
4. Concatenation is the process of connecting together two or more strings **[1]**, linking them together as one **[1]**
5. Example:

```
string1 = input("What is your first name?")        [1]
string2 = input("What is your last name?")
string3 = input("What year were you born?")
userName = string1,[0] + string2,[0] + string3     [2]
    print(userName)                                [1]
end
```

6. Example:

```
myFile = openRead("story.txt")        [1]
lineOne = myFile.readLine()           [1]
print(lineOne)                        [1]
myFile.close()                        [1]
```

Programming Techniques 2

1. To save time **[1]**, to avoid repetitive code **[1]** and to organise/structure programs **[1]**
2. a) 5 **[1]**
   b) 6 **[1]**
   c) More than one colour could begin with the same letter **[1]**
   d) bikeID **[1]**
3. a) SELECT bikeID FROM Stock WHERE colourCode = "G"; **[1]**
   b) SELECT bikeID FROM Stock WHERE numberofGears > 20; **[1]**
   c) SELECT bikeID FROM Stock WHERE numberofGears = 18 AND inStock = "Yes"; **[1]**

Programming Techniques 3

1. a) Example:

```
array laptime[4]        [1]
laptime[0] = "59.4"     [1]
laptime[1] = "64.3"
laptime[2] = "74.3"
laptime[3] = "81.9"
```

   b) By adding the times of several runners **[1]**

2. Parameters refer to variables within a sub-program **[1]**, and arguments are the actual data passed to the parameters **[1]**
3. a) Example:

```
function conversion()                               [1]
    cTemp = input("Enter the temperature in C")     [1]
    fTemp = cTemp * 1.8 + 32                         [1]
return(fTemp)                                        [1]
endfunction
```

   b) A function will return a value; a procedure will not **[1]**

Producing Robust Programs

1.

Normal data	Acceptable, error-free data likely to be input into the program.
Boundary data	Values at the limit of what a program should be able to accept.
Invalid data	Values of the correct data type but that cannot be processed as they are outside pre-determined limits.
Erroneous data	Incorrect data of a type that should be rejected by the program or system.

[3]

2. a) Making sure to consider all those who will be using your program **[1]** and what access each user will be given **[1]**
   b) Examples: use of usernames and passwords **[1]**; making sure children have access to relevant areas only **[1]**; considering what might happen when incorrect keys are pressed **[1]**
3. Use of comments within the program **[1]**; use of indentation **[1]**; use of well-named variables **[1]**; use of sub-programs **[1]**
4. Syntax errors break the rules of the language and will prevent a program from running **[1]**; a program with a logic error will run but provide an unexpected result **[1]**
5. A logic error may be written correctly without any syntax errors **[1]** but references between lines of code may be confused and can often only be spotted by working through the program one line at a time **[1]**.
6. Boundary data tests the ranges of expected values that may be entered **[1]** and erroneous data considers incorrect entries that should not be processed **[1]**.

Languages, Translators and Integrated Development Environment

1. Examples: Python **[1]**; C Family **[1]**; Java **[1]**; JavaScript **[1]**; Visual Basic **[1]**; PHP **[1]**; Delphi **[1]**; SQL **[1]**; Bash **[1]**
2. Any two of the following: they may prefer the fine control and lower memory usage **[1]**; they may specifically want to focus on CPU processing **[1]**; they may be working with older devices **[1]**
3. Code is colour coded, visually highlighting errors **[1]** and language-specific coding mistakes are highlighted when the program is run **[1]**
4. The program can be run virtually before being translated **[1]**; data type errors can be spotted **[1]**; sections of program can be run and checked **[1]**

Answers

5.

Editors	These are designed for writing source code, with tools to assist with formatting and syntax.
Error diagnostics	Also known as debugging tools, these will help to identify errors in particular lines of code.
Run-time environment	This allows programs to be run virtually within the IDE software.
Translators	These will compile or interpret the final code as required.

[3]

6. Compilers **[1]** convert whole programs to machine code **[1]**. Interpreters **[1]** convert one line of code at a time to machine code **[1]**.

Pages 188–197 Paper 1: Computer Systems

1. a) The remote storing and accessing of files and applications via the Internet **[1]**
   b) i) Two advantages from the following: files can be accessed from any Internet-connected location **[1]**; additional storage devices do not need to be carried **[1]**; access to files can be shared with other users **[1]**
      ii) Two disadvantages from the following: loss of access if Internet connection is lost **[1]**; speed of access is determined by Internet connection **[1]**; access is not available in all geographical areas **[1]**
   c) Primary storage describes the main memory of the computer **[1]**
      Any example from: RAM **[1]**; ROM **[1]**; CPU Cache **[1]**. Secondary storage devices are seperate from the CPU and motherboard **[1]**
      Any example from: Hard drive **[1]**; Optical disk (or example of) **[1]**; SSD (or example of) **[1]**
2. a) Two reasons from the following: to update security settings **[1]**; to add functionality **[1]**; to update drivers **[1]**
   b) i) Random access memory is a temporary area that a computer uses to store data and instructions in current use **[1]**
      ii) Additional RAM means more short-term memory to carry out tasks **[1]**, allowing the processor to run and perform better **[1]**
   c) i) Additional short-term memory space created by the CPU on the hard drive if RAM becomes full **[1]**
      ii) Advantage: creates additional RAM without replacing or adding hardware **[1]**. Disadvantage: removes storage space from the hard disk **[1]** OR access to virtual memory is not as fast as RAM **[1]**
      iii) Files are moved OR grouped together **[1]**; empty spaces are grouped together **[1]**
3. a) i) Local area network. Computers are connected with the ability to share data in a small geographical area **[1]**

      ii) A router is needed to connect them **[1]**. A WAN could be created **[1]**.
   b) i) Any three of the following: Wired Equivalent Privacy (WEP) **[1]**; Wi-Fi Protected Access (WPA) **[1]**; Wi-Fi Protected Access 2 (WPA2) **[1]**; Wi-Fi Protected Access 3 (WPA3) **[1]**
      ii) WPA3 **[1]**, as it is the most recent and most secure **[1]**
   c) These standards allow components and operating systems from around the world **[1]** to communicate/function with each other **[1]**
4. a) i) Copyright, Designs and Patents Act 1988 **[1]**
      ii) The Data Protection Act 2018 **[1]**
   b) i) Lossy compression permanently removes data from files **[1]**, whereas lossless uses an algorithm to compress data but then reconstructs it without data loss **[1]**.
      ii) Lossless **[1]** should be used to preserve all original elements after editing **[1]**
   c) Analogue audio is converted to a digital format using sampling **[1]** and the higher the sample rate **[1]** and bit depth **[1]**, the higher the quality.
5. a) i) The search for vulnerabilities within a system that could be exploited for criminal purposes **[1]**
      ii) User access levels are used to control the information that a specific user, or groups of users, can access, read or edit **[1]**
   b) i) Three reasons from the following: landfill is growing around the world **[1]**; the computers could be used by another user **[1]**; chemicals and hard-to-recycle elements can damage the environment **[1]**; creating new products increases greenhouse gases **[1]**; the transportation of products and waste causes pollution **[1]**
      ii) One alternative from the following: charities will repurpose machines so that they can be given to those without access **[1]**; the equipment can be passed on to educational establishments **[1]**
6. a) To flood a website or network with data traffic so that it is brought to a halt **[1]**
   b) Three pieces of advice from the following: make sure that passwords are at least eight characters long **[1]**; use upper- and lower-case characters **[1]**; include special characters (for example ?, # and %) **[1]**; avoid using real dictionary words **[1]**; avoid using any personal information **[1]**; regularly change passwords **[1]**; never use the same password for more than one system **[1]**
   c) i) HTTP Secure encrypts communication between server and client **[1]**
      ii) A set of rules to allow multiple network devices around the world to communicate **[1]**
   d) Three from the following: virus **[1]** – a program hidden within another program or file, designed to cause damage to file systems **[1]**; worm **[1]** – a malicious program that acts independently and can replicate itself and spread throughout a system **[1]**; Trojan **[1]** – installed by a user who thinks that it is a legitimate piece of software when, in fact, it will cause damage or provide access to criminals **[1]**; spyware **[1]** – secretly passes information on to a criminal without your knowledge and is often packaged with free software **[1]**; adware **[1]** – displays targeted advertising and redirects search requests without permission **[1]**;

Answers

ransomware [1] – limits or denies a user access to their system until a ransom is paid to unlock it [1]; pharming [1] – the redirecting of a user's website – by modifying their DNS entries – to a fraudulent site without their permission [1]

7. a) Server 3 [1], as it has the highest number of cores [1] and the largest hard drive space [1]
    b) Two advantages from the following: the failure of one device, as long as it is not the server, will not affect the rest of the network [1]; the network can be expanded by adding devices until the server capacity is reached [1]; localised problems can be identified quickly [1]; data can be directed to a specific address via the central server, reducing traffic [1]
    Two disadvantages from the following: if the server fails, then the whole network will collapse [1]; extensive cabling is required [1]; a high level of technical knowledge is required to maintain the server [1]
    c) Software can be installed remotely on client machines by the network manager [1]; low-specification client machines can be added or replaced at low cost as required [1]; security and network access can be controlled from the network's central location [1]

8. a) Data is converted into a meaningless form that cannot be read [1] without the decryption key [1]
    b) i) Scams, or similar techniques, designed to steal personal information [1]
       ii) Phishing (or variation of) via email or messaging [1]; shouldering – trying to look at a PIN [1]; blagging – trying to con someone face-to-face [1]

9. Mark Band 3 – High Level (6–8 marks)
    Level of detail:
    Thorough knowledge and understanding. Wide range of considerations in relation to question. Response is accurate and detailed. Application of knowledge with evidence/examples related to question. Both sides of discussion carefully considered.
    Mark Band 2 – Mid Level (3–5 marks)
    Level of detail:
    Reasonable knowledge and understanding. Range of considerations in relation to question. Response is generally accurate. Application of knowledge relates to content. Discussion of most areas.
    Mark Band 1 – Low Level (1–2 marks)
    Level of detail:
    Basic knowledge and understanding. Limited consideration in relation to question with basic responses. Limited application of knowledge and basic discussion of content.
    Content should include any of the following:
    * Physical security
      * Use of locks, safe rooms or obstacles
      * Removable hard drives
      * Increased surveillance
      * Biometric scanners: fingerprints, iris, facial, voice
    * Online security
      * Use of firewalls to prevent external access
      * Anti-malware/spyware software
      * User access levels – not allowing access outside of a role
      * Use of strong/regularly changing/non-repeated passwords

* Use of encryption to prevent access to data even if stolen
* Legislation
  * Data Protection Act – ensuring that details are secure and up to date
  * Computer Misuse Act – accessing secure information and sharing or using it to commit crime

Pages 198–209 **Paper 2: Computational Thinking, Algorithms and Programming**

Section A

1. a) A record is a single row or entry of related data in a database [1]; a field is a database category within a record [1]
    b) i)
    ```
    SELECT * FROM VipCustomers WHERE
    carsBought == 1;
    ```
    [1]
       ii)
    ```
    SELECT firstName FROM VipCustomers
    WHERE carsBought >= 3;
    ```
    [1]
       iii)
    ```
    SELECT firstName, surname, contactNumber
    FROM VipCustomers WHERE postCode ==
    "VC2 4RD";
    ```
    [1]

2. a) 13, 32, 10, 19 (original) > 13, 10, 32, 19 > 13, 10, 19, 32 > 10, 13, 19, 32 > 10, 13, 19, 32 (final) [3]
    b) Check the first item 10 = 13 False, check the second item 10 = 32 False, check the third item 10 = 10 Correct [3]
    c) Binary search [1]

3. a) i) Example:
    ```
    goalsScored [3,4]
    ```
    [1]
    ```
    goalsScored = [["12", "3","3","2"],["13",
    "2","4","5"],["14","6","4","7"]]
    ```
    [2]
    (1 mark for first line; 2 marks for second line)
       ii) Example:
    ```
    goalsScored
    [1,3]
    ```
    [1]
    b) A one-dimensional array can only hold a single list of common elements OR a two-dimensional array can hold more than one list [1]

4. a) i)
    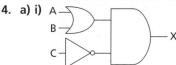

    (1 mark for each shape in correct location) [Total 3]

Answers

ii)

A	B	C	X
0	0	0	0
0	0	1	0
0	1	0	1
0	1	1	0
1	0	0	1
1	0	1	0
1	1	0	1
1	1	1	0

(1 mark for each row) [Total 8]

b) Both inputs A AND B must be turned off **[1]** to produce a positive output at Z **[1]**

5. a) Binary sequence: 01101001 10010110 **[1]**

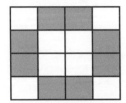

(1 mark for each line) [Total 5]

b) 16 **[1]**

c) One each from the following:
Advantage: files can be downloaded quickly **[1]**;
small file sizes mean less storage capacity is used **[1]**
Disadvantage: quality/fine detail can be lost **[1]**;
original image cannot be restored **[1]** [Total 2]

6. a) TB **[1]**
b) 11111001 **[1]**
c) 259 doesn't fit into 8 bits, so the computer tries to process more bits than it is designed to handle **[1]**
d) 10011110 **[1]**, 158 **[1]**
e) E = 1110, 9 = 1001, 11101001 = 233 **[2]**

7. a) Example:

```
string1 = input("Please enter your mobile
number")
        if (string1,[0]) = 0
replace (string1,[0]) with (+44) then
        print("Your international number is" +
string1)
else
        print("Number not recognised")
endif
```

**(1 mark – input; 1 mark – string; 1 mark – if;
1 mark – replace number; 1 mark – else)** [Total 5]

b) String **[1]**

Section B

8. a) i) diceOne **[1]**, diceTwo **[1]**
   ii) Asking the question **[1]** is diceOne exactly equal to diceTwo? **[1]**

b)

Data Type	Tick one box
String	
Integer	✓ **[1]**
Real	
Boolean	

Explanation: Dice numbers are only whole numbers from 1–6 **[1]**

c) i) Function **[1]** as it returns a calculated value **[1]**
   ii) Example:

```
function diceRoll()
diceOne = random(1,6)
diceTwo = random(1,6)
if diceOne == diceTwo then
        print("Start the game")
else
        print("Next person")
endif
return diceRoll
end function
```

(1 mark – use of correct variables; 1 mark – use of procedure; 1 mark – use of random function correctly; 1 mark – use of print) [Total 4]

d)

Test Data	Test Type	Expected Result
diceOne = 2 diceTwo = 3	Normal	Roll again
diceOne = 1 diceTwo = 6	Boundary	Roll again **[1]**
diceOne = 9 diceTwo = 7	Invalid **[1]**	Roll again **[1]**
diceOne = 4 diceTwo = 4	Normal **[1]**	Start game **[1]**

Answers

e) i)

Line	Input (TempC)	tempF	Output
1	10 **[1]**	-	-
2	-	18 **[1]**	-
3	-	50 **[1]**	-
4	-	-	50 **[1]**

ii)

```
tempC = input("Please enter the temperature in
Celsius")
tempF = tempC * 1.8
tempC = tempC + 32
if tempF > averageTemp then
        print(tempF + "is above average")
elseif tempF == averageTemp then
        print(tempF + "is average")
elseif tempF < averageTemp then
        print(tempF + "is below average")
else
        print("error")
endif
```

**(1 mark – use of correct variables; 1 mark – use
of if/else; 1 mark – use of Boolean logic; 1 mark –
use of print)**   **[Total 4]**

f)

```
minutesUsed = input("Input minutes used")
if minutesUsed > 180
        print("You've exceeded your daily limit")
else
        print("You are still under your daily limit")
endif
```

**(1 mark – use of correct variables; 1 mark – use of if/
else; 1 mark – use of Boolean logic; 1 mark – use of
print)**   **[Total 4]**

Notes

Notes

Acknowledgements

The author and publisher are grateful to the copyright holders for permission to use quoted materials and images.

All images © Shutterstock.com

Every effort has been made to trace copyright holders and obtain their permission for the use of copyright material. The author and publisher will gladly receive information enabling them to rectify any error or omission in subsequent editions. All facts are correct at time of going to press.

Published by Collins
An imprint of HarperCollins*Publishers* Ltd
1 London Bridge Street
London SE1 9GF

HarperCollins*Publishers*
Macken House
39/40 Mayor Street Upper
Dublin 1
D01 C9W8
Ireland

ISBN 978-0-00-853523-0

First published 2022

10 9 8 7 6 5 4 3 2

British Library Cataloguing in Publication Data.

A CIP record of this book is available from the British Library.

Author: Paul Clowrey
Publisher: Clare Souza
Project management and editorial: Charlotte Christensen, Chantal Addy and Richard Toms
Reviewing: Adam Gibson
Cover Design: Kevin Robbins and Sarah Duxbury
Inside Concept Design: Sarah Duxbury and Paul Oates
Text Design and Layout: Jouve India Private Limited
Production: Karen Nulty
Printed in India by Multivista Global Pvt. Ltd.

This book contains FSC™ certified paper and other controlled sources to ensure responsible forest management.

For more information visit: www.harpercollins.co.uk/green